Full Stack AngularJS for Java Developers

Build a Full-Featured Web Application from Scratch Using AngularJS with Spring RESTful

Ravi Kant Soni

Apress®

Full Stack AngularJS for Java Developers

Ravi Kant Soni
Bangalore, Maharashtra, India

ISBN-13 (pbk): 978-1-4842-3197-5   ISBN-13 (electronic): 978-1-4842-3198-2
https://doi.org/10.1007/978-1-4842-3198-2

Library of Congress Control Number: 2017962309

Cover image by Freepik (`www.freepik.com`).

Managing Director: Welmoed Spahr
Editorial Director: Todd Green
Acquisitions Editor: Pramila Balan
Development Editor: Laura Berendson
Technical Reviewer: Abhishek Satyam
Coordinating Editor: Prachi Mehta
Copy Editor: Kim Wimpsett

Distributed to the book trade worldwide by Springer Science+Business Media New York, 233 Spring Street, 6th Floor, New York, NY 10013. Phone 1-800-SPRINGER, fax (201) 348-4505, e-mail orders-ny@springer-sbm.com, or visit `www.springeronline.com`. Apress Media, LLC is a California LLC and the sole member (owner) is Springer Science + Business Media Finance Inc (SSBM Finance Inc). SSBM Finance Inc is a **Delaware** corporation.

For information on translations, please e-mail rights@apress.com, or visit `www.apress.com/rights-permissions`.

Apress titles may be purchased in bulk for academic, corporate, or promotional use. eBook versions and licenses are also available for most titles. For more information, reference our Print and eBook Bulk Sales web page at `www.apress.com/bulk-sales`.

Any source code or other supplementary material referenced by the author in this book is available to readers on GitHub via the book's product page, located at `www.apress.com/978-1-4842-3197-5`. For more detailed information, please visit `www.apress.com/source-code`.

Printed on acid-free paper

To my Papa

Sri Ras Bihari Prasad

&

To my Maa

Smt. Manorma Devi

I love you, Papa and Maa. Without your true love and warmest support, the completion of this book would not have been possible.

To my Beautiful & Beloved Wife

Mrs. Soniya Singh

*Without whom I would be nothing. You always comfort and console,
never complain or interfere, ask nothing, and endure all.*

I love you my sweetheart, Soniya.

Contents

About the Author

Ravi Kant Soni, an affable and determinant gentleman from Lashkariganj (near "Sher Shah Suri" Tomb), Sasaram, Bihar (India), is a Full Stack Java Application Developer and published author of the 2 books 'Learning Spring Application Development' and 'Spring: Developing Java Applications for the Enterprise'. Adding to his attainment, he has completed his graduation bachelor degree (B.E) in Information Science & Engineering from Reva University, Bangalore (India), and schooling from Bal Vikash Vidyalaya, Sasaram, Bihar (India).

Ravi has worn many hats throughout his tenure, ranging from software development to multi-tenant application design to integration of new technology into an existing system to his all time love of writing a book. Ravi has focused on Full Stack Web Application Development for most of his career and has been extensively involved in application design and implementation. He has developed applications for Banking System, HR & Payroll System and e-Commerce systems and also gained recognition by the management for his designing abilities for a premium program.

Along with the above accomplishment, Ravi takes pride for his present status in both professional and personal life. His Charisma does not end here and his achievement yet has wide spectrum with his well-versed experience in all aspects of software engineering, including software design, systems architecture, application programming and automation testing.

The Gentleman has encountered various hurdles that unlocked his potential and made him grow as a better human being setting productive goals and simultaneously achieving the same. Ravi loves problem statements and enjoys brainstorming unique solutions. Contact this self-driven, Competent and amazing Team-Player at HYPERLINK ravikantsoni.author@gmail.com. You can also get in touch with him at https://www.linkedin.com/in/november03ravikantsoni/.

About the Technical Reviewer

Abhishek Satyam works as a technical lead and architect at IBM India Pvt Ltd based in Bangalore, Karnataka. He has more than six years of experience with databases, data warehouses, analytics, big data, APIs, enterprise web applications, Python, and artificial intelligence.

A graduate in computing from Staffordshire University in the United Kingdom, Satyam has a long record of successfully leading multiple enterprise assignments at IBM and was awarded the IBM Eminence and Excellence award from Ginni Rometty, CEO of IBM Corp, for a Watson cognitive assignment in 2016. In 2012 and 2013, he was decorated with the Best Employee Award from IBM.

Satyam is a multifaceted data management professional whose specific areas of expertise are in data management, programming, algorithms, analytics, big data, cloud SaaS/PaaS, UI/UX, and SEO where he currently has ten professional certifications. He also has extensive knowledge in cloud infrastructure and enterprise application enablement of leading cloud-centric ecosystems such as Amazon Web Services (AWS) and IBM Bluemix.

Currently he is leading his department's efforts on IBM Watson, cognitive application development, machine learning, and Internet of Things.

Acknowledgments

Writing a technical book involves fathomless research, review, support, and most preciously my time when I have full-time job. Here's thanking all those who helped me on this book:

First of all, I would like to thank Goddess 'Maa Tara Chandi' for giving me so much.

Without my families' love, strong support, and understanding this book would have remained a virtual commodity. My profound thanks to my family – my mother Smt. Manorma Devi and my father Sri Ras Bihari Prasad, my mama Suresh Soni & Naresh kashyap, my in-laws Sri Jai Narayan Singh & Smt. Pramila Devi – for their love and support, during the writing of this book.

My Special Thanks goes to a man who has been a rock of stability throughout my life and whose loving spirit sustains me still - my uncle Sri. Arun Kumar Soni for the great inspiration he has given me to achieve all success in life, and also special thank to my aunt Smt. Ranju Devi.

My Thanks also goes to my beloved wife Mrs. Soniya Singh, the person after my parents who I am thank for making my life beautiful is you.

Thanks also to my dearest brothers Shashi Kant and Shree Kant, my sweetest sister Namrata Soni- who has always loved me. My thanks also to my cousins Komal, Chulbili, Bhulchuli, Rishi and Mittu.

And thanks also to Saurabh Kumar Singh and Pinky Singh.

My deepest gratitude and appreciation goes to my dearest friend, Awanish Kumar, IAS – District Magistrate at Nicobar District, Andaman and Nicobar Island; who wants and encourages my knowledge to come out on paper to ignite others. Thanks also to my dearest friend Alok Kumar - Software Engineer 4 at Cisco; and Nagendra Kumar – Engineering Lead at Facebook Inc. for giving me positive thoughts which work as a fuel to carry on.

I would like to thank the Apress publishing crew for helping me and having the utmost professionalism. Special thanks to Laura Berendson, development editor, and Prachi Mehta, coordinating editor, for their knowledge that spans an amazing spectrum and without whom this book wouldn't have been possible.

My heartfelt thanks go to the reviewers commissioned by Apress for their valuable input.

Last but not least, I am thankful to everyone who supported me in one or another in writing this book.

Welcome to *Full Stack AngularJS for Java Developer*.

—Ravi Kant Soni

■ ■ ■

CHAPTER 1

The Big Picture of Full Stack Web Development

Full stack web development lets you explore the best tools and frameworks while making your application solid and reliable on different fronts such as design, scalability, robustness, and security.

In this chapter, I will cover the big picture of full stack web development and discuss the architecture of modern applications to overcome the myth that developing isolated desktop and mobile applications is a good approach. I will discuss AngularJS as a front-end framework and Spring Boot as a back-end framework. I will also show how to set up Spring Boot as the development environment. Then you will develop your first Spring Boot application and run this application. Finally, you will monitor your Spring Boot application using the Spring Boot actuator.

What Is a Full Stack Developer?

Whenever someone tells you they are a full stack developer, the first question you will probably ask is, "What kind of full stack developer are you?" The thing is, when you work with the Web today, you have to use lots of tools. The *stack* has become larger than what it was before.

Companies nowadays prefer to employ engineers who are flexible enough to do anything rather than have a lot of expertise with just one technology. The final goal is that you will be able to code Java, use Angular, write database scripts, write CSS, and so on. In fact, a few years ago, it was easy to say that you were a full stack developer, but today you will have to take care of Java, AngularJS, Bootstrap, CSS, database scripts, and several databases, and also you will need to know about content delivery, deployment, and how to publish to an Amazon Web Services cluster. Needless to say, it is complicated to manage all of this at once. And I haven't even mentioned areas such as designing the UI and creating mobile applications. So, there is a lot to know when you say you are full stack developer.

Is a full stack developer the one who knows a little bit about all these subjects or has a mastery of all of them? Many times, full stack developers are considered to be jacks-of-all-trades but masters of none. So, it's best to decide on what kind of full stack developer you are.

Being a full stack developer means you need to pretty much become a connector. So, even if you have one set of good skills, you can prep your work for delivery so that another person can do their work at the other end and know how to receive it. That's where full stack developers are very valuable.

But the chances of finding a good full stack developer are extremely low. The thing is, startup companies always need a full stack developer who can look into all things, and startups are always desperate to hire full stack developers for any amount of money.

© Ravi Kant Soni 2017
R. K. Soni, *Full Stack AngularJS for Java Developers*, https://doi.org/10.1007/978-1-4842-3198-2_1

The definition of a full stack developer in the industry is an engineer who is specialized in everything from client-side coding such as HTML, CSS, and AngularJS to the server side such as Java and Spring Boot and is experienced with different databases, including both RDBMS and NoSQL database systems. So, a full stack web developer should have good hands-on experience with both client-side and server-side technologies, as shown in Figure 1-1.

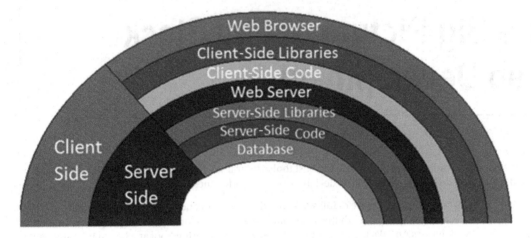

Figure 1-1. *Client-side and server-side technologies*

The full stack developer is responsible for getting every part of the system to run smoothly. The developer should have expertise in the following:

- Designing user interfaces

- Developing business logic and service layers on the server side

- Handling relational and nonrelational databases

- Handling API interaction

- Securing applications using authentication and authorization programmatically

- Ensuring quality assurance

- Understanding business requirements and customer needs

In addition to all this, a full stack developer must know how to do basic server management, providing the roles of a server admin or DevOps when necessary.

- Connecting to the cloud server through a command or terminal and access tools like putty

- Managing sets and subsets of users and groups

- Doing basic shell scripting in a designated server environment

- Understanding the Apache and Nginx server programs

- Managing firewall and permissions

- Installing, updating, and managing server-side software, packages, and libraries

In addition, with the evolution of cloud infrastructure, a full stack developer should be aware of the platform as a service (PaaS) and software as a service (SaaS) models, Amazon Web Services, and IBM Bluemix.

This section was all about being a full stack web developer. Let's dig into the big picture of full stack development in the next section.

Full Stack Web Development

The *stack* is the combination of tools and components that make up an application. In a web application, the components can be on the front end (HTML, CSS, JavaScript/jQuery) or the back end (server operations, logical layers, and databases). Note that today the database can be placed in a separate section instead of the server-side operation because of database as a service (DaaS).

Full stack web development means being comfortable working with both front-end and back-end technologies. Put simply, full stack development covers client-side development using HTML/CSS, JavaScript/jQuery, and framework such as AngularJS and Bootstrap.

For server-side development, it covers programming languages such as Java, frameworks such as Spring Boot, databases such as PostgreSQL or Oracle or any other database, and everything in between.

The communication between the client side and the server side happens through a RESTful API and HTTP, as shown in Figure 1-2. Let's discuss the architecture of modern web applications in the next section.

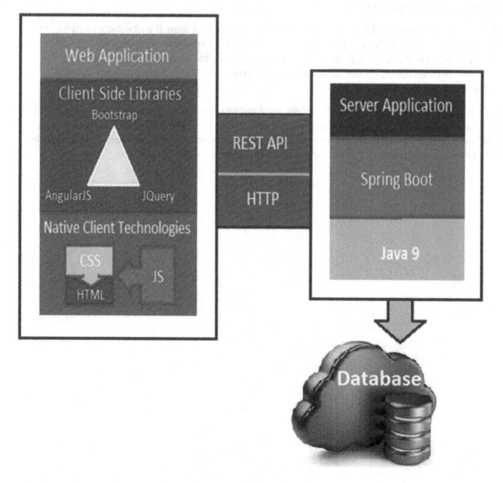

Figure 1-2. Communication between the client and server

Architecture of Modern Web Applications

In the early days of the Web, web applications didn't exist. We had web sites full of static content and images. There were advantages and disadvantages to this.

Here are a few advantages:

- There was very low computational overhead on the server.

- The content itself was highly cacheable as the data was static and didn't change for lots of ISPs and server providers.

Here are a few disadvantages:

- It was hard to update content.

- There was no personalization, and everybody got the same experience.

- The UI was usually poor when compared to the applications of today.

CGI introduced a revolution by enabling dynamic content creation using scripting languages. On the downside, there was a relatively high computational overhead, and it required you to be an expert in HTML and scripting languages on the server side.

Then JavaScript came, which enabled the pages to be dynamic for the first time. It was mostly used for very basic scripting to validate forms or display pop-up ads. It enhanced the usability and reduced round-trips to server for very basic validations. The disadvantage was that you had to implement the business logic twice, once on the client side and once on the server side. So, we have come up with the architecture of modern web applications.

In this section, I will discuss the architecture of modern applications to overcome the myth that developing isolated desktop and mobile applications is a good way to go. Modern web applications focus on a distributed back-end infrastructure to serve content and front-end clients over the Web using RESTful APIs, as shown in the layered architecture of the web application in Figure 1-3.

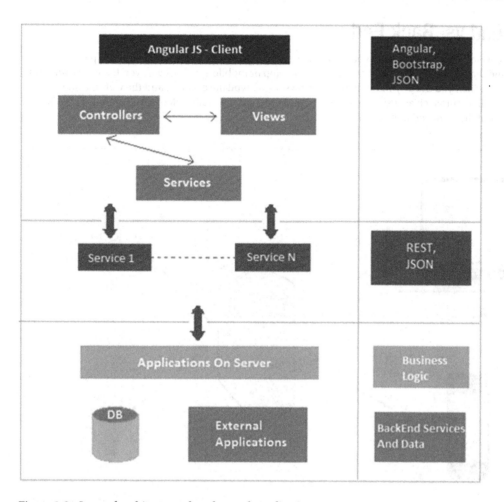

Figure 1-3. *Layered architecture of modern web applications*

When you want to interact with multiple components on a page and those components have many more intermediate components, then it is hard for all the intermediate components to implement server-side rendering. Compared to the traditional server-side architecture, the main idea here is to build the server as a set of stateless reusable REST services. From the Model-View-Controller (MVC) point of view, the controller has been taken out of the back end and moved onto the client. So, now the client is capable of using the MVC architecture. The client has a separate view layer that contains all the presentation logic. It also has a separate front-end services layer and a controller layer.

During the initial startup of an application, only the JSON data is transferred between the client and server using a RESTful API. The entire business logic will be exposed as REST endpoints that will be consumed by Angular services. The benefit here is that when you have a mobile app of your web application, you can just consume the RESTful services without writing any additional code on the server side for your mobile app.

REST stands for Representational State Transfer, which is an architectural style that is an abstraction opposed to a concrete thing. It is the architecture of the Web as it works today. You will study RESTful APIs in more detail in Chapter 2 where you will be creating the RESTful layer for your application.

Front End vs. Back End

When you develop a web application, you separate the development process mainly into two parts: the front end and the back end. When you talk about a web app or mobile app, basically you focus on front-end development. When you use any web app or any browser, you type the address, and the web site opens with multiple elements such as text, images, forms, and different interactive elements. Figure 1-4 shows the physical view of the front end and back end.

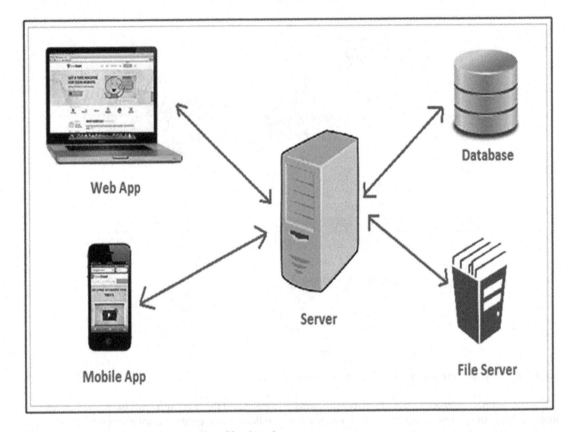

Figure 1-4. *Physical view of front end and back end*

If you use a mobile app, you will have different elements, list views, and so on. These applications will appear on the client side. So, whether you have a laptop or mobile device or you are using a browser or mobile application, you will get the client side of a complete application.

All the user data is stored in a database. All the business logic and secured data are stored on the server. The server receives requests from the web app or mobile app, processes these requests, grabs the necessary information from the database or the files from the file server, and sends them back to the front-end app. So basically, the back end stores the information, and the front end displays the information.

Designers and developers commonly use a framework for prototyping web sites and applications because building an app or web site from scratch takes a lot of time.

The software framework is defined as *software framework* is predefined set of reusable modules that can be implemented to accomplish a designated job better and faster. Thus, a software framework always contains libraries, compilers, and multiple APIs to develop a specific enterprise web application. A good full stack developer should know which framework is most appropriate to implement for their set of applications.

These are a few of the popular software frameworks available:

- AngularJS (for UI/front-end development)

- Ionic (for hybrid mobile app prototyping and development)

- Pure MVC framework (application development framework)

- Selenium (web testing framework)

In computer programming, a software framework is an abstraction in which software providing generic functionality can be selectively changed by additional user-written code, thus providing application-specific software.

Front-End Framework

The front end involves everything that the user sees, including the design and some languages like HTML and CSS. The main aim of the front-end code is to interact with the user, as well as present the data in a well-defined style.

There are so many amazing JavaScript libraries that you can use when building a front-end application. Sometimes it can be a bit tricky to choose one single project. The front end is all the stuff that makes the web application look and feel sexy. This front-end content is HTML, CSS, and JavaScript. You will use AngularJS as a front-end development framework in this book. I'll cover AngularJS in more detail later in the chapter.

AngularJS as a Front-End Framework

AngularJS is a library written in JavaScript for web application development. It addresses the challenges of a single-page application (SPA). An AngularJS web application follows the MVC design pattern that results in developing extendable, maintainable, testable, and standardized web applications. AngularJS data binding and dependency injection make it an ideal partner with any server technology because it eliminates much of the code you would otherwise have to write, and it all happens within the browser.

AngularJS Version

AngularJS is commonly referred to as Angular.js or sometimes as AngularJS 1.*x*. AngularJS is a JavaScript-based open source front-end web application development framework and is mainly maintained by Google.

Now, Angular 4.0.0 is available and is backward compatible with 2.*x.x* for most applications. This new version contains some new features such as an animation package pulled out from core into its own package, an improved ngIf that supports if/else style, and more.

AngularJS Architecture Concepts

Now you will take a look at the architecture concepts of AngularJS. When an HTML document is loaded into the browser and is evaluated by the browser, the following happens:

1. The AngularJS JavaScript file is loaded, and the Angular global object is created. The JavaScript file that registers the controller functions is executed.

2. AngularJS scans the HTML to look for AngularJS apps and views and finds a controller function corresponding to the view.

3. AngularJS executes the controller functions and updates the views with data from the model populated by the controller.

4. AngularJS listens for browser events, such as button clicked, mouse moved, input field being changed, and so on. If any of these events happen, then AngularJS will update the view accordingly.

Figure 1-5 shows a workflow diagram of AngularJS.

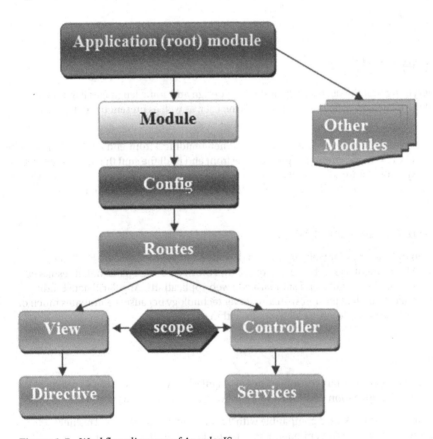

Figure 1-5. *Workflow diagram of AngularJS*

AngularJS contains modules that act as containers for different types of applications such as views, controllers, directives, services, and so on. A module specifies how an application can be bootstrapped. Then you have a config component.

The routes are used for linking URLs to controllers and views. A view is used to handle a sophisticated event. It uses ng-view directives. The controller controls the data of the AngularJS application, which consists of regular JavaScript objects. AngularJS defines an ng-controller directive that creates new controller objects by using the controller function.

AngularJS comes with several built-in services such as $http, $route, $window, $location, and so on. The *scope* consists of objects that refer to the model. They play the important role of joining the controller with the view. We will discuss these in more detail in Chapter 3.

MVC Architecture

AngularJS uses an MVC architecture to create web applications. The MVC architecture is a programming methodology that aims to split an application into three core components: a model, a view, and a controller. These three components combine to form your application. Figure 1-6 shows the Model-View-Controller architecture.

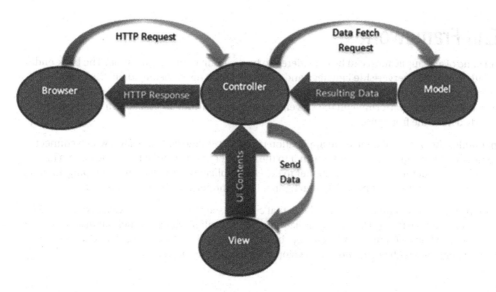

Figure 1-6. *MVC architecture in AngularJS*

When a user sends an HTTP request via a browser, the request is received by the controller.
The controller processes that request and sends the request to the model to provide the appropriate data. The model in response provides the resulting data array to the controller again. The controller processes the data again to the required format and sends it to the view. The view represents the data via UI contents and sends it to the controller. Finally, the controller sends the HTTP response to the browser.

- *AngularJS views* are used to generate an output representation of information, such as a chart or a diagram, to the user in a web browser. AngularJS builds the views in the document object model (DOM) by pulling in all the templates defined for an application. So, the developer work here is to just create the template by using mostly HTML and CSS.

- The *AngularJS model* contains the $scope object that is used to store the application model, so there's no need to create a JavaScript model class like with other JavaScript client-side frameworks. Scopes are attached to the DOM, helping to simplify the JavaScript problem considerably.

- The *AngularJS controller* is the place where you define all the business logic specific to a particular view. The controller holds the model and view together.

Twitter Bootstrap

Twitter Bootstrap is a front-end framework that was created to make responsive design much easier. The Bootstrap CSS framework can be used to style the content of a web site. You can create your own CSS style to make your web site look awesome, but Bootstrap provides a nice set of CSS styles that will let you design a really great-looking content layout. It is not really required to use Bootstrap while working with AngularJS, and there is no intrinsic relationship between AngularJS and Bootstrap as both are different packages.

To use CSS from the Bootstrap CSS framework, you can define a dependency in pom.xml while developing a Spring Boot application so that it will be automatically downloaded to the library folder. Also, you can download the Bootstrap archive from https://getbootstrap.com/, which also contains CSS and JavaScript files.

Back-End Framework

The back-end code of any application can be considered to be the brain of that application. The back-end code is built with the use of a server-side language and database and is never visible to the user. The front-end code interacts with the end user in real time, and anything displayed on the web site inside the browser is because of a query performed on the server, where back-end code interacts with the server to return user-ready data to the front end.

The developer builds the back-end code of an application using server-side code like Java, which connects with the database to save or update data and return it to the end user in the form of front-end code. This kind of back-end code structure helps the developer to develop applications to do online shopping, interact socially, look for real-time information, and do much more in the modern world of the Internet.

There are so many frameworks and libraries available that can be used to make the back-end coding much simpler and the performance faster. The most popular one that you will be using throughout this book is the Spring Framework. The Spring Framework has always been popular for building the back-end features in enterprise applications, and with Spring Boot, a developer's life has never been easier.

Spring Boot as a Back-End Framework

Why Spring Boot? There are lots of frameworks for developing web applications, and Spring Boot is just one of them. If you want to build something fast, Spring Boot can be the first choice as a web application development framework.

> *Working with Spring Boot is like pair programming with the Spring developers.*
>
> —By Josh Long @starbuxman

The team at Pivotal has designed a new lightweight framework named Spring Boot to ease the bootstrapping and development of stand-alone Spring-based and production-ready applications and services with minimum fuss that you can "just run."

Spring Framework Problems and Spring Boot Advantages

Let's understand some of the Spring Framework's problems. Spring Framework was mostly about dependency injection in 2006. Later it grew and became a whole application framework that lets you build enterprise Java applications. It addresses most of the business logic such as handling transactions by providing templates to create an easy-to-build enterprise application.

The Spring Framework also has a configuration module where Spring handles lots of common concerns such as handling HTTP requests, connecting to databases, and so on, and it allows the developer to focus on business services. The developer develops business services and annotates classes with Spring-provided annotations, which lets Spring know about those services. Spring also has infrastructure support such as connecting to an RDBMS database or a MongoDB database.

But while bringing these features, Spring also brings some problems such as it is a huge framework that has multiple setup and configuration steps. There are multiple build and deploy steps.

To address these problems, Spring Boot came into the picture. Spring Boot abstracts these steps and allows developers to once again focus on the business logic. Spring Boot's main aim is to address the complexity of configuration in the Spring Framework by taking most of the work out of configuring Spring-based applications; there is no need for XML or code configuration most of the time.

Another interesting feature that Spring Boot provides is "no WAR, only JAR." So, you don't have to generate a WAR file and then upload it to a Tomcat server; you can create self-hosted web applications and execute them as Java JAR applications, making the deployment extremely easy and straightforward.

Spring Boot has opinions, which means Spring Boot has reasonable defaults. You can build an application quickly using these commonly used values. Spring Boot automatically configures the required classes depending on the libraries on its classpath.

Suppose your application wants to interact with the database. If there are Spring Data libraries on a class path, then Spring Data automatically sets up a connection to a database along with the data source class. Since Tomcat is a popular web container, by default a Spring Boot web application uses an embedded Tomcat container.

With Spring Boot, you can expose components such as REST services independently, the same as proposed in the microservices architecture, so that when maintaining any of the components, you no longer have to redeploy the entire system.

Primary Goals of Spring Boot

The following are the primary goals of Spring Boot:

- To provide production-ready applications and services with minimum fuss that anyone can "just run."

- To be opinionated, which means making certain decisions for developers and supporting ranges of nonfunctional features that are common for enterprise applications (embedded servers, security, health checks, metrics, and externalized configuration)

- To support convention over configuration, avoid XML configuration completely, and avoid annotation configuration

- To allow developers to customize Spring Boot applications to their liking

Develop Your First Spring Boot Application

In this section, you will develop your first Spring Boot application step by step. If you are already familiar with this process, you can skip to the end to see how it all fits together. There are different options for starting a new project. For more details, refer to `https://spring.io/`.

System Requirements

Spring Boot 2.0.0.M2 requires Java 8. So, the first thing that is required is the Java 8 SDK. If you have already set up the JDK in your system, you should check the current version of Java installed on your system before you begin.

```
$ java -version
java version "1.8.0_101"
Java(TM) SE Runtime Environment (build 1.8.0_101-b13)
Java HotSpot(TM) 64-Bit Server VM (build 25.101-b13, mixed mode)
```

The Spring team has provided the following three approaches to create a Spring Boot application using the opinionated approach:

- Using the Spring Boot CLI tool
- Using the Spring STS IDE
- Using Spring Initializr (`http://start.spring.io/`)

A developer can develop Spring Boot Groovy applications using the Spring Boot CLI, Spring STS IDE, or Spring Initializr web site. They can develop Spring Boot Java applications using the Spring STS IDE or Spring Initializr web site.

Using the Spring Boot CLI

Spring Boot has a command-line interface that lets developer create Spring Boot applications. I will not be covering this topic in this book; for information about it, you can refer to `http://docs.spring.io/spring-boot/docs/2.0.0.M2/reference/htmlsingle/#getting-started-installing-the-cli`.

Using Spring Initializr

To start a new Spring Boot project from absolutely nothing, you can create a new project from the web service called Spring Initializr provided by Spring Boot: `http://start.spring.io/`. By entering the required information and selecting a set of desired options (dependencies), you can download either a build file project or a zipped file project that contains a standard Maven or Gradle project in the root directory.

This lets you bootstrap an application by choosing options and downloading it. You can select the type of project such as Maven or Gradle, and you can select the version for Spring Boot. Also, you can select Project Metadata, as shown in Figure 1-7.

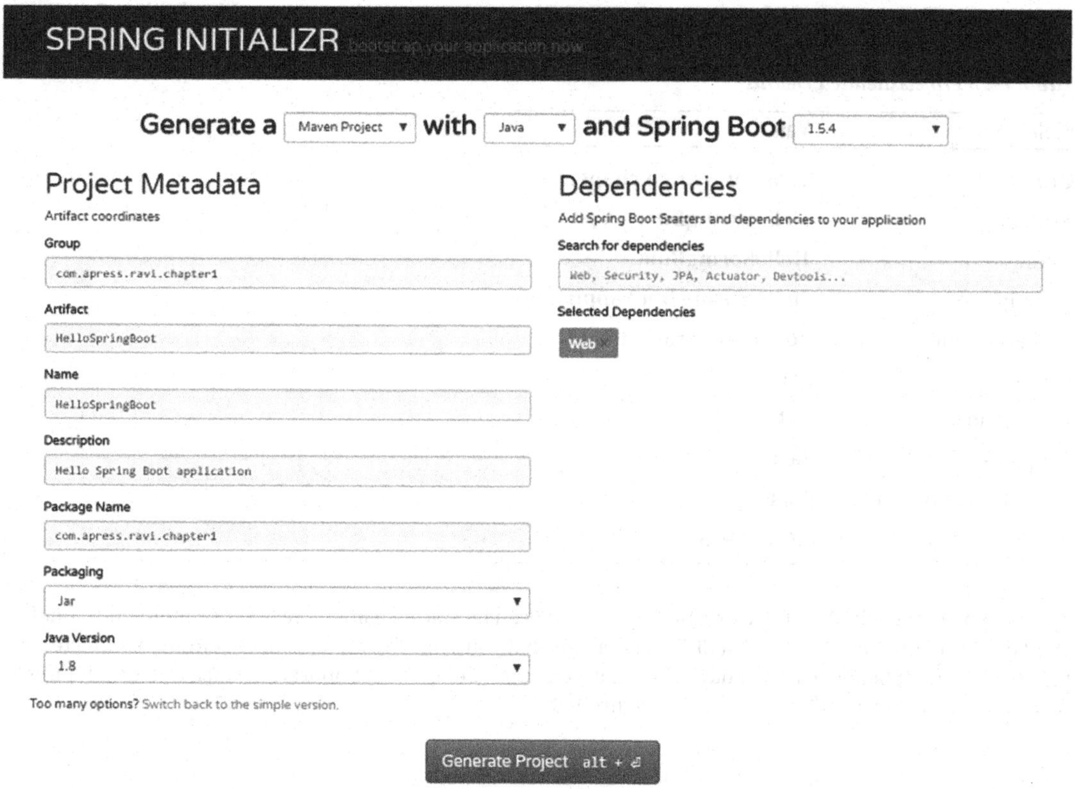

Figure 1-7. *Spring Initializr*

You will be developing a Maven project in this book.

The screen in Figure 1-7 is a bit long so was cut off. Table 1-1 shows you all the settings for this example.

***Table 1-1.** Project-Related Details*

Field	Value
Group	**com.apress.ravi.chapter1**
Artifact	**HelloSpringBoot**
Name	**HelloSpringBoot**
Description	**Hello Spring Boot application**
Package Name	**com.apress.ravi.chapter1**
Packaging	**Jar**
Java Version	**1.8**
Language	**Java**
Project dependencies	**Web**
Generate a	**Maven Project**

Spring Boot lets developers create executable JARs that can be started using `java -jar` or more traditional WAR deployments. You can get a list of dependencies that you select based on your requirements. To create the HelloSpringBoot application, I have chosen a web dependency that supports full stack web development with Tomcat and Spring MVC, as shown in Figure 1-8.

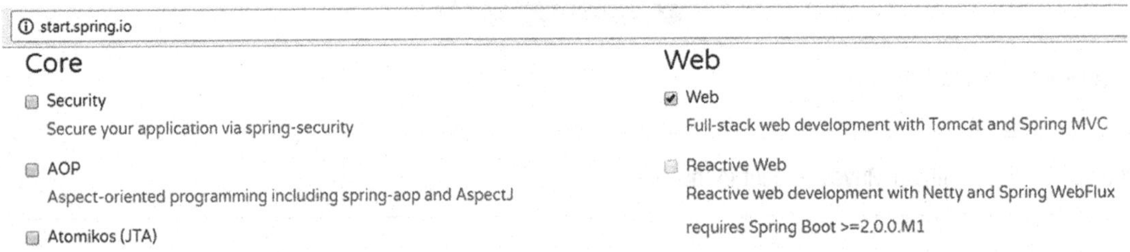

***Figure 1-8.** Web dependency in Spring Initializr*

Click the Generate Project button to download the `HelloSpringBoot.zip` file. You can import a Maven project (after unzipping it) directly into the Spring Source Tool (STS) and work your way through it from there.

I will be using STS as an IDE throughout this book. If you don't have STS installed yet, visit `https://spring.io/tools/sts/all` and download a copy for your operating system. To install it, simply unpack the downloaded archive. When you're done, go ahead and launch STS.

Another option for creating a Spring Boot project is to use a wizard by selecting File ➤ New ➤ Spring Starter Project.

Using Spring Tool Suite

The Spring Tool Suite comes as a ready-to-use distribution of the latest Eclipse releases with the Spring IDE components pre-installed. Use a Spring Starter Project wizard to create a basic Spring Boot application (Figure 1-9).

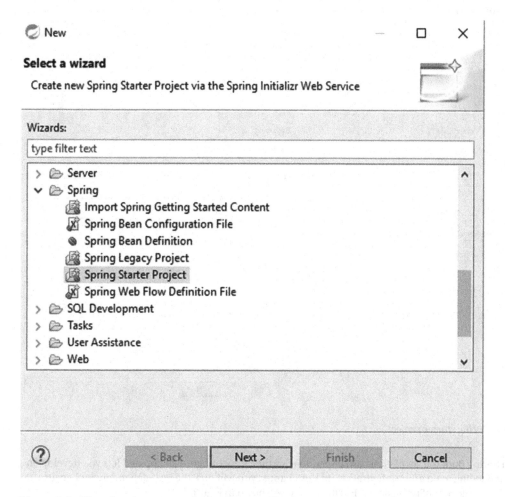

Figure 1-9. *The wizard to create a Spring Boot application*

Spring Boot provides so-called *starters* where you need to provide project-related details, as shown in Figure 1-10.

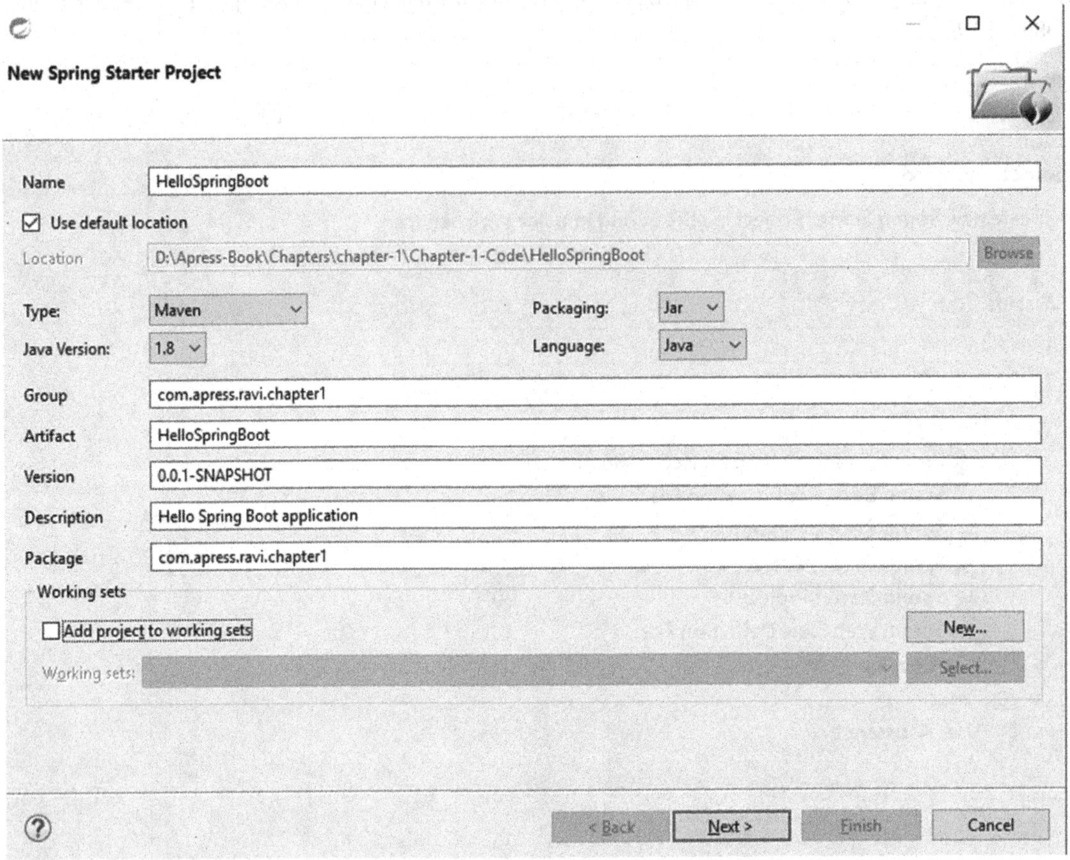

Figure 1-10. Spring starter project

A starter in Spring Boot is a set of classpath dependencies that autoconfigure an app and lets you develop an app without needing to do any configuration. In this chapter, you will pick the web dependencies because you'll build a simple HelloSpringBoot RESTful service, as shown in Figure 1-11.

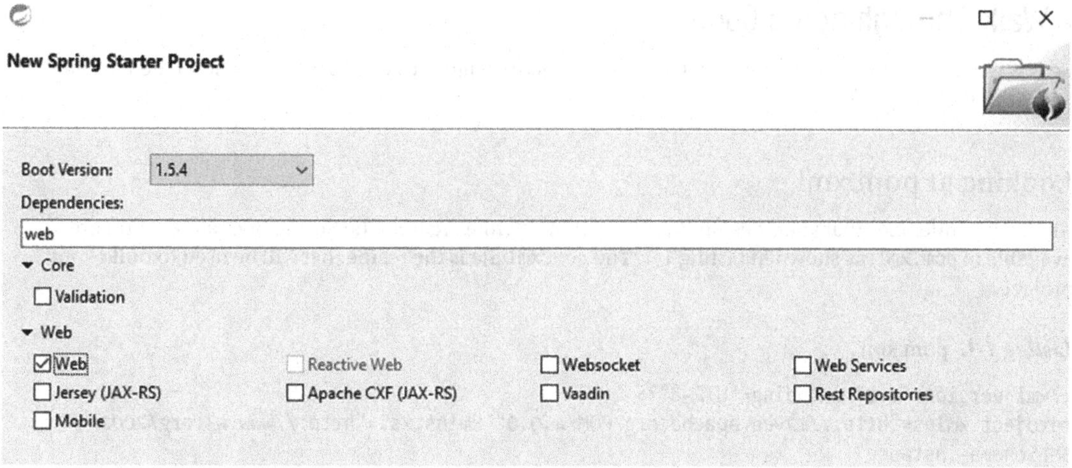

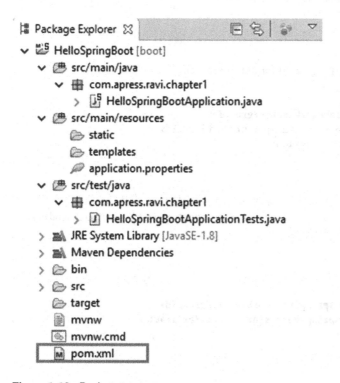

Figure 1-11. *Selecting a web dependency in the Spring starter*

Clicking the Finish button will generate a workspace where you can create a new package and class and static files in your resources. The final structure of the project will look like Figure 1-12.

Figure 1-12. *Project structure*

Let's go through the code in the next section.

A Walk-Through of the Code

Let's walk through the code for more details. You will go through the code in pom.xml and in the Java files. Let's start with pom.xml.

Looking at pom.xml

All the dependencies that you select in the starter dialog while creating the Spring Boot application are available in pom.xml, as shown in Listing 1-1. The pom.xml file is the recipe that will be used to build your project.

Listing 1-1. pom.xml

```xml
<?xml version="1.0" encoding="UTF-8"?>
<project xmlns="http://maven.apache.org/POM/4.0.0" xmlns:xsi="http://www.w3.org/2001/
XMLSchema-instance"
        xsi:schemaLocation="http://maven.apache.org/POM/4.0.0 http://maven.apache.org/xsd/
        maven-4.0.0.xsd">
        <modelVersion>4.0.0</modelVersion>

        <groupId>com.apress.ravi.chapter1</groupId>
        <artifactId>HelloSpringBoot</artifactId>
        <version>0.0.1-SNAPSHOT</version>
        <packaging>jar</packaging>

        <name>HelloSpringBoot</name>
        <description>Hello Spring Boot application</description>

        <parent>
                <groupId>org.springframework.boot</groupId>
                <artifactId>spring-boot-starter-parent</artifactId>
                <version>1.5.4.RELEASE</version>
        </parent>

        <properties>
                <project.build.sourceEncoding>UTF-8</project.build.sourceEncoding>
                <project.reporting.outputEncoding>UTF-8</project.reporting.outputEncoding>
                <java.version>1.8</java.version>
        </properties>

        <dependencies>
                <dependency>
                        <groupId>org.springframework.boot</groupId>
                        <artifactId>spring-boot-starter-web</artifactId>
                </dependency>
```

```
        <dependency>
                <groupId>org.springframework.boot</groupId>
                <artifactId>spring-boot-starter-test</artifactId>
                <scope>test</scope>
        </dependency>
    </dependencies>

    <build>
        <plugins>
            <plugin>
                    <groupId>org.springframework.boot</groupId>
                    <artifactId>spring-boot-maven-plugin</artifactId>
            </plugin>
        </plugins>
    </build>
</project>
```

Note the following about Listing 1-1:

- The `<parent>` element specifies the Spring Boot parent POM, which contains definitions for common components.

- The `<dependency>` element on `spring-boot-starter-web` tells Spring Boot that the application is a web application and lets Spring Boot form its opinions accordingly.

Before going further, let's understand Spring Boot's opinions. You need to understand how Spring Boot uses a starter like `spring-boot-starter-web` to form its configuration opinions. The HelloSpringBoot application uses `spring-boot-starter-web` as Spring Boot's web application starter. Based on this starter, Spring Boot has formed the following opinions:

- Spring MVC for the REST framework

- Apache Jackson for the JSON binding

- Tomcat embedded web server container

- Hibernate for object-relational mapping

After Spring Boot forms an opinion about the type of application you intend to build, Spring Boot delivers a set of Maven dependencies based on the POM contents and starter specified for the HelloSpringBoot application. Figure 1-13 shows some of the Maven dependencies that Spring Boot has set up in STS.

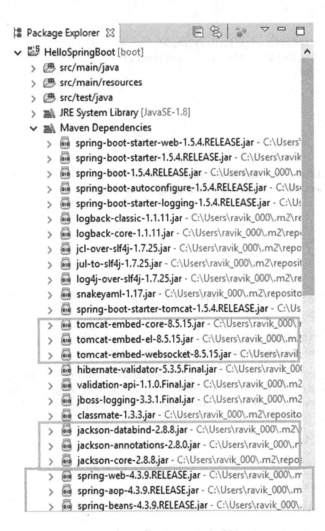

Figure 1-13. *Maven dependencies set up in STS*

You can see in Figure 1-13 that Tomcat is the default embedded web server container. Suppose you want to use Jetty instead of Tomcat; all you need to do is change the <dependencies> section in the POM, as shown in Listing 1-2.

Listing 1-2. pom.xml with Dependency for Tomcat and Jetty

```
<dependency>
        <groupId>org.springframework.boot</groupId>
        <artifactId>spring-boot-starter-web</artifactId>
        <exclusions>
                <exclusion>
                        <groupId>org.springframework.boot</groupId>
                        <artifactId>spring-boot-starter-tomcat</artifactId>
                </exclusion>
        </exclusions>
</dependency>
```

```
<dependency>
        <groupId>org.springframework.boot</groupId>
        <artifactId>spring-boot-starter-jetty</artifactId>
</dependency>
```

You can see in Figure 1-14 that the Maven dependencies for Tomcat are replaced with dependencies for Jetty.

Figure 1-14. *Updated Maven dependencies*

Writing the Code

To bootstrap a Spring Boot application, you can start from a `main()` method. Most likely you can just delegate to the `static SpringApplication.run` method, as shown in Listing 1-3.

Listing 1-3. com.apress.ravi.chapter1.HelloSpringBootApplication.java

```
package com.apress.ravi.chapter1;

import org.springframework.boot.SpringApplication;
import org.springframework.boot.autoconfigure.SpringBootApplication;
import org.springframework.web.bind.annotation.RequestMapping;
import org.springframework.web.bind.annotation.RestController;
/**
 * @author RaviKantSoni
 */
@SpringBootApplication
@RestController
public class HelloSpringBootApplication {

        public static void main(String[] args) {
                SpringApplication.run(HelloSpringBootApplication.class, args);
        }

        @RequestMapping("/hello")
        public String greeting(){
                return "Hello World!";
        }
}
```

Let's step through the important parts.

@SpringBootApplication Annotation

The first annotation of the `HelloSpringBootApplication` class is `@SpringBootApplication`. The `@SpringBootApplication` annotation is a convenience annotation introduced in Spring Boot 1.2.0 and adds the following annotations:

- `@Configuration`: A class annotated with the `@Configuration` annotation can be used by the Spring container as a source of bean definitions, which is not specific to Spring Boot. This class may contain one or more Spring bean declarations by annotated methods with the `@Bean` annotation.

- `@EnableAutoConfiguration`: This annotation is part of the Spring Boot project that tells Spring Boot to start adding the beans using classpath definitions or settings. Autoconfiguration intelligently guesses and configures beans that you are likely to run with the application and thus simplifies the developer's work.

    - For example, let's assume you have `tomcat-embedded.jar` on your classpath, and then you want a `TomcatEmbeddedServletContainerFactory` bean to configure the Tomcat server. So, this will be automatically searched for and configured without any manual XML configurations.

- Normally, for a Spring MVC application, you add the @EnableWebMvc annotation, which flags the application as a web application and activates key features such as setting up a DispatcherServlet, but Spring Boot will automatically add this annotation when it sees spring-webmvc on the classpath. Similarly, the @EnableTransactionManagement annotation will be automatically added, which will enable declarative transaction management.

- @ComponentScan: This annotation tells Spring to look for specific packages to scan for annotated components, configurations, and services.

@RestController and @RequestMapping Annotations

The first annotation of the HelloSpringBootApplication class is @RestController, which is a *stereotype* annotation. The @RequestMapping annotation provides "routing" information and tells Spring that any HTTP request with the path /hello should be mapped to the greeting method.

The @RestController and @RequestMapping annotations come from Spring MVC (these annotations are not specific to Spring Boot).

The main Method

The main part of the HelloSpringBootApplication class is the main method. The Spring application developed using Spring Boot contains the main method, which calls Spring Boot's SpringApplication.run() method to launch an application, as shown in the previous code. The class that contains a main method is referred to as the *main class* and is annotated with the @SpringBootApplication annotation.

Running a Spring Boot Application in STS

The Spring Boot application created using the Spring Starter Project wizard comes in two flavors: WAR and JAR. This wizard allows you to choose between WAR and JAR in its packaging option.

> As Josh Long said in one of his talks in the Spring IO, "Make JAR, not WAR."
>
> —https://twitter.com/springcentral/status/598910532008062976

Spring Boot favors JARs over WARs by allowing you to easily create stand-alone JAR packaged projects that add an embedded web server (Apache Tomcat is the default web server) inside the created artifact, and it helps developers reduce the overhead of setting up local or remote Tomcat servers, WAR packaging, and deploying.

To run the Spring Boot application locally, you don't need any special tooling from STS. You just need to run it by selecting Run As ➤ Java Application, either from the standard Eclipse Java debugging tools or from STS.

The benefits of using STS over IDEs are that it provides a dedicated launcher, which does the same thing as an IDE but adds a few useful bells and whistles on the top of that. So, let's use STS to run the Spring Boot application, as shown in Figure 1-15.

Right-click the project fullstackdeveloper and select Run As ➤ Spring Boot App.

Figure 1-15. *Wizard in STS to run application*

The Spring Boot application starts with some output in the console, as shown in Figure 1-16.

Figure 1-16. *Output on the console*

If the application starts successfully, the last line of the console output from Spring Boot will contain the words *Started HelloSpringBootApplication*.

Congratulations! You have successfully set up and run the application using Spring Boot. Now it's time to visit http://localhost:8080/hello in the browser to see the web page, as shown in Figure 1-17.

Hello World!

Figure 1-17. *Accessing the REST endpoint from the browser*

Starters

Starters are a set of convenient dependency descriptors that you can include in your application. They contain a lot of dependencies that you need to get your project up and running quickly. The starter POMs are dependency descriptors that can be added to your application's Maven.

In simple words, if you are developing a project that uses Spring MVC for HTTP request processing, you just have to include `spring-boot-starter-web`, which will import all the required dependencies for the Spring MVC application such as `view-resolver`, `tomcat`, and so on. This reduces the burden of configuring all the required dependencies for a framework.

You can refer to `http://docs.spring.io/spring-boot/docs/2.0.0.M2/reference/htmlsingle/#using-boot-starter` for a complete list of starters.

Spring Boot Actuator: Production-Ready Features

Spring Boot has a bunch of features that let you monitor your Spring Boot application in production or any environment after you deploy it. For example, you can get logs, perform thread dumps, view metrics, analyze garbage collection, and show beans configured in `BeanFactory`. This information can be exposed via HTTP or JMX, and it even can be logged into the process via SSH.

Enabling Actuator

Actuator HTTP endpoints are available only to Spring MVC. This is a new endpoint that gets added to your application without you writing a controller. The definition of an *actuator* is a production-ready feature to help you monitor and manage your application.

The simplest way to enable the production-ready feature is to add the `spring-boot-actuator` module dependency `spring-boot-starter-actuator` from the Spring starter, as shown in Figure 1-18.

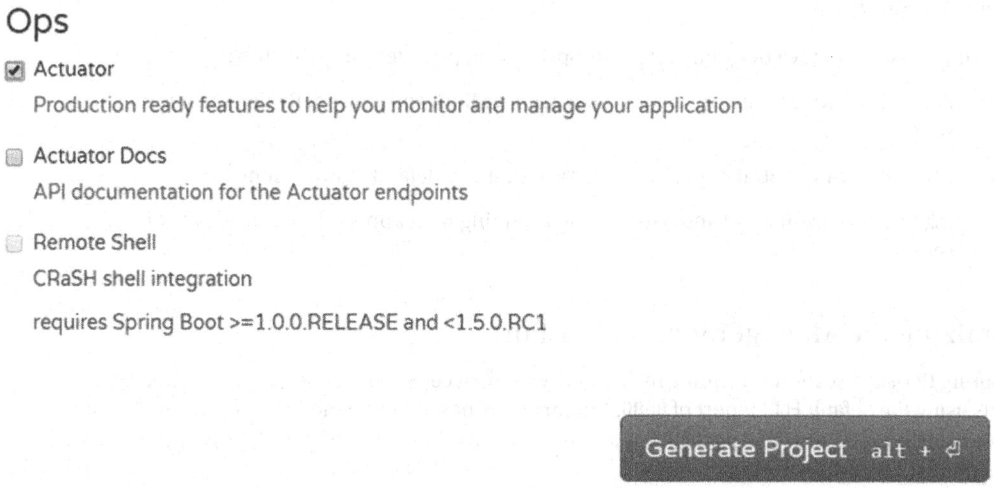

Ops

☑ Actuator

Production ready features to help you monitor and manage your application

▢ Actuator Docs

API documentation for the Actuator endpoints

▢ Remote Shell

CRaSH shell integration

requires Spring Boot >=1.0.0.RELEASE and <1.5.0.RC1

Generate Project alt + ↵

Figure 1-18. Actuator dependency in Spring Initializr

To add the actuator to a Maven-based project, add the following `starter` dependency in `pom.xml`:

```
<dependency>
    <groupId>org.springframework.boot</groupId>
    <artifactId>spring-boot-starter-actuator</artifactId>
</dependency>
```

Running the Application

Once you run the Spring Boot application, the actuator endpoints will be logged in the console, as shown in Figure 1-19.

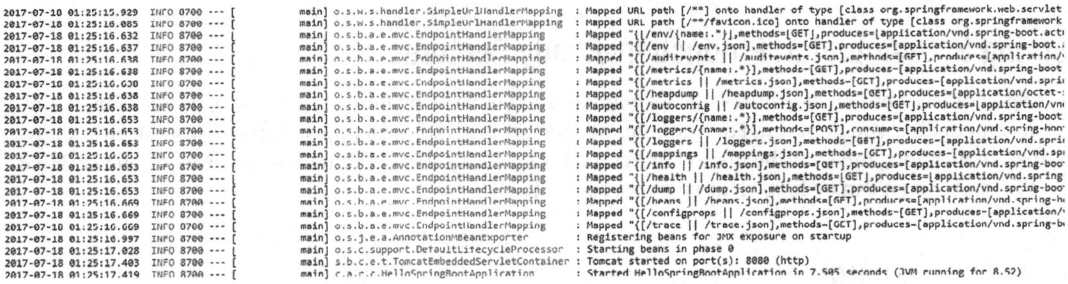

```
2017-07-18 01:25:15.929 INFO 8700 --- [ main] o.s.w.s.handler.SimpleUrlHandlerMapping : Mapped URL path [/**] onto handler of type [class org.springframework.web.servlet
2017-07-18 01:25:16.085 INFO 8700 --- [ main] o.s.w.s.handler.SimpleUrlHandlerMapping : Mapped URL path [/**/favicon.ico] onto handler of type [class org.springframework
2017-07-18 01:25:16.632 INFO 8700 --- [ main] o.s.b.a.e.mvc.EndpointHandlerMapping    : Mapped "{[/env/{name:.*}],methods=[GET],produces=[application/vnd.spring-boot.act
2017-07-18 01:25:16.637 INFO 8700 --- [ main] o.s.b.a.e.mvc.EndpointHandlerMapping    : Mapped "{[/env || /env.json],methods=[GET],produces=[application/vnd.spring-boot.
2017-07-18 01:25:16.638 INFO 8700 --- [ main] o.s.b.a.e.mvc.EndpointHandlerMapping    : Mapped "{[/auditevents || /auditevents.json],methods=[GET],produces=[application/
2017-07-18 01:25:16.638 INFO 8700 --- [ main] o.s.b.a.e.mvc.EndpointHandlerMapping    : Mapped "{[/metrics/{name:.*}],methods=[GET],produces=[application/vnd.spring-boot
2017-07-18 01:25:16.638 INFO 8700 --- [ main] o.s.b.a.e.mvc.EndpointHandlerMapping    : Mapped "{[/metrics || /metrics.json],methods=[GET],produces=[application/vnd.spri
2017-07-18 01:25:16.638 INFO 8700 --- [ main] o.s.b.a.e.mvc.EndpointHandlerMapping    : Mapped "{[/heapdump || /heapdump.json],methods=[GET],produces=[application/octet-
2017-07-18 01:25:16.638 INFO 8700 --- [ main] o.s.b.a.e.mvc.EndpointHandlerMapping    : Mapped "{[/autoconfig || /autoconfig.json],methods=[GET],produces=[application/vn
2017-07-18 01:25:16.653 INFO 8700 --- [ main] o.s.b.a.e.mvc.EndpointHandlerMapping    : Mapped "{[/loggers/{name:.*}],methods=[GET],produces=[application/vnd.spring-boot
2017-07-18 01:25:16.653 INFO 8700 --- [ main] o.s.b.a.e.mvc.EndpointHandlerMapping    : Mapped "{[/loggers/{name:.*}],methods=[POST],consumes=[application/vnd.spring-boo
2017-07-18 01:25:16.653 INFO 8700 --- [ main] o.s.b.a.e.mvc.EndpointHandlerMapping    : Mapped "{[/loggers || /loggers.json],methods=[GET],produces=[application/vnd.spri
2017-07-18 01:25:16.653 INFO 8700 --- [ main] o.s.b.a.e.mvc.EndpointHandlerMapping    : Mapped "{[/mappings || /mappings.json],methods=[GET],produces=[application/vnd.sp
2017-07-18 01:25:16.653 INFO 8700 --- [ main] o.s.b.a.e.mvc.EndpointHandlerMapping    : Mapped "{[/info || /info.json],methods=[GET],produces=[application/vnd.spring-boo
2017-07-18 01:25:16.653 INFO 8700 --- [ main] o.s.b.a.e.mvc.EndpointHandlerMapping    : Mapped "{[/health || /health.json],methods=[GET],produces=[application/vnd.spring
2017-07-18 01:25:16.653 INFO 8700 --- [ main] o.s.b.a.e.mvc.EndpointHandlerMapping    : Mapped "{[/dump || /dump.json],methods=[GET],produces=[application/vnd.spring-boo
2017-07-18 01:25:16.669 INFO 8700 --- [ main] o.s.b.a.e.mvc.EndpointHandlerMapping    : Mapped "{[/beans || /beans.json],methods=[GET],produces=[application/vnd.spring-b
2017-07-18 01:25:16.669 INFO 8700 --- [ main] o.s.b.a.e.mvc.EndpointHandlerMapping    : Mapped "{[/configprops || /configprops.json],methods=[GET],produces=[application/
2017-07-18 01:25:16.669 INFO 8700 --- [ main] o.s.b.a.e.mvc.EndpointHandlerMapping    : Mapped "{[/trace || /trace.json],methods=[GET],produces=[application/vnd.spring-b
2017-07-18 01:25:16.997 INFO 8700 --- [ main] o.s.j.e.a.AnnotationMBeanExporter       : Registering beans for JMX exposure on startup
2017-07-18 01:25:17.028 INFO 8700 --- [ main] o.s.c.support.DefaultLifecycleProcessor : Starting beans in phase 0
2017-07-18 01:25:17.403 INFO 8700 --- [ main] s.b.c.e.t.TomcatEmbeddedServletContainer : Tomcat started on port(s): 8080 (http)
2017-07-18 01:25:17.419 INFO 8700 --- [ main] c.a.r.c.HelloSpringBootApplication      : Started HelloSpringBootApplication in 7.505 seconds (JVM running for 8.52)
```

Figure 1-19. *Actuator endpoints in console log*

Using Actuator Endpoints

Spring Boot includes a number of actuator endpoints, which allow you to monitor and interact with your Spring Boot application. Most of the endpoints are sensitive, and they are not fully public, while a few are not such as `/health` and `/info`.

The following are some of the common endpoints Spring Boot provides out of the box:

- `/health` shows health information for a running Boot application. By default, it is not sensitive.
- `/Info` displays arbitrary application information. By default, it is not sensitive.
- `/metrics` shows metrics information for a running Boot application. By default, it is sensitive.

Customizing the Management Server Port

If your Spring Boot application is running inside your own data center, then you may prefer to expose endpoints using the default HTTP port of 8080. But for cloud-based deployments, exposing management endpoints using the default HTTP port 8080 is a sensible choice. The `management.port` property can be used to change the HTTP port.

You can assign port number 8081 to the `management.port` property using `src\main\resources\application.properties file: management.port=8081.`

Getting Health Information

The /health endpoint can be used to check the health/status of your running Spring Boot application. It returns a JSON file with a bunch of matrixes. Going to http://localhost:8081/health in the browser will give the results shown in Figure 1-20.

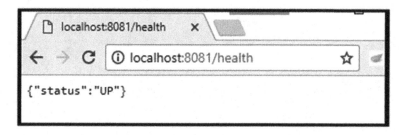

Figure 1-20. *Accessing the /health endpoint*

The following health information is shown to unauthorized access over HTTP:

```
{
        "status":"UP"
}
```

In Chapter 7, I will discuss the Spring Boot actuator in more detail so you can understand what this returned JSON data represents.

Summary

In this chapter, you got an over of what a full stack developer is and what full stack web development entails. You also learned about the architecture of modern web applications. You got an overview of AngularJS as a front-end framework and Spring Boot as a back-end framework. You developed your first Spring Boot application. Finally, you learned how to monitor your Spring Boot application using an actuator. In the next chapter, you will create a RESTful application using Spring Boot to perform the CRUD operations.

CHAPTER 2

■ ■ ■

Creating the RESTful Layer for Your Application

In the previous chapter, you got the big-picture view of full stack web development. You also looked at the fundamentals of Spring Boot and created a HelloWorld REST application using Spring Boot. In this chapter, you will learn about the following:

- REST

- Building RESTful services

- Handling errors in a RESTful API

Now it's time to develop a more complex RESTful application using Spring Boot. To develop any RESTful service, you must first understand RESTful APIs and know how to implement them. So, I will first introduce REST and the RESTful API concept and then walk you through the code for developing a RESTful API.

This should be enough to get you started exploring all the different possibilities when it comes to RESTful API design and implementation. Let's start with an introduction to REST.

Introduction to REST

Representational State Transfer (REST) is an architectural style that describes how one system communicates or shares state with another system. The fundamental concept of REST is a resource, which is anything that can be accessed or manipulated. These states need to be represented using a common format such as XML or JSON. In the case of web applications, HTTP is commonly used to support a RESTful architecture. In other words, REST is used to create a web application that exposes an HTTP API.

HTTP Methods and CRUD Operations

Standard HTTP methods such as GET, POST, PUT, and DELETE are used to access and manipulate REST web resources. The CRUD operations have four basic persistent functions: create, read, update, and delete. Table 2-1 shows the mapping of CRUD operations to the four HTTP verbs.

© Ravi Kant Soni 2017
R. K. Soni, *Full Stack AngularJS for Java Developers*, https://doi.org/10.1007/978-1-4842-3198-2_2

Table 2-1. *Mapping of CRUD Operations to HTTP Verbs*

CRUD Operation	HTTP Method	Description
Create	POST	Performs a create operation
Read	GET	Performs a read operation
Update	PUT	Performs an update operation
Delete	DELETE	Performs a delete operation

HTTP Status Codes

The meaningful HTTP status codes help clients utilize your RESTful API. Table 2-2 lists some HTTP status code elements that might be returned as the server response when calling a RESTful API.

Table 2-2. *HTTP Status Codes*

Code	Message	Description
200	OK	The request has succeeded (this is a standard response for a successful HTTP request).
201	Created	The request has been fulfilled, and the request successfully created a new resource.
204	Not Content	The request has processed successfully but is not returning any content.
400	Bad Request	The request could not be fulfilled because of bad syntax.
401	Unauthorized	The request requires user authorization.
403	Forbidden	The server refuses to fulfill the request.
404	Not Found	The requested resource could not be found.
409	Conflict	The request cannot be completed because of a resource conflict.

Refer to Appendix A to learn about some tools you can use to access RESTful applications to test RESTful APIs. I will be using Postman from Chrome as the REST client throughout this book.

Build a RESTful Service: UserRegistrationSystem

In this chapter, you will be building a RESTful application called UserRegistrationSystem with REST endpoints for user registration. I will be referring to this as the *base* application throughout this book.

Introducing UserRegistrationSystem

UserRegistrationSystem can be understood as a software as a service (SaaS) provider, which allows the user to perform CRUD operations such as creating a new user, getting a list of all users, getting individual users, updating a user, and deleting a user.

UserRegistrationSystem will be formed with a REST API layer and a repository layer, with a domain layer crosscutting those two, which gives a separation of concerns. The REST API layer is responsible for handling client requests, validating client input, interacting with the repository layer (or service layer), and generating a response.

The domain layer contains a domain object that has business data. The repository layer interacts with the database and supports CRUD operations. You will begin the development of your RESTful service by understanding these requirements:

- Consumers register themselves by creating a new user.

- A list of users can be obtained.

- Individual user details can be obtained.

- User details can be updated at the later time.

- A user can be deleted when required.

Identifying REST Endpoints

A URI endpoint is used to identify REST resources. The name you choose for the UserRegistrationSystem REST API endpoint should have a clearly defined meaning to consumers. To design endpoints for services, you should follow some best practices and conventions that are widely used in the software industry.

- Use a base URI for the RESTful API to provide an entry point.

- Name resource endpoints using plural nouns.

- Use a URI hierarchy to represent related resources.

The UserRegistrationSystem application will have a User resource. This User resource can be accessed using the GET, POST, PUT, and DELETE HTTP methods. Table 2-3 lists the REST endpoints you will be creating for your application.

Table 2-3. REST Endpoint for UserRegistration

HTTP Method	REST Endpoint	Description
GET	/api/user/	Returns the list of users
GET	/api/user/{id}	Returns user details for the given user {id}
POST	/api/user/	Creates a new user from POST data
PUT	/api/user/{id}	Updates the details of the given User {id}
DELETE	/api/user	Deletes a user for the given user {id}

The next step is to define a resource representation and the representation format. REST typically supports multiple formats such as HTML, JSON, and XML. In this chapter, and the rest of the book, JSON will be the preferred format for the API operation.

JSON Format

JavaScript Object Notation (JSON) is a syntax for storing and exchanging data between the client and the server. A JSON object is a key-value data format where each key-value pair consists of a key in double quotes followed by a colon (:), followed by a value. JSON objects are surrounded by curly braces ({}) where each key value is separated by a comma (,). Listing 2-1 shows an example of a User JSON object.

Listing 2-1. User JSON Object

```
{
        "id": 1,
        "name":"Ravi Kant Soni",
        "address":"Lashkariganj, Sasaram, Rohtas, Bihar, pin-821115",
        "email":"ravikantsoni.author@gmail.com"
}
```

As you can see, a User resource has a name, address, and e-mail as the key, and the id attribute uniquely identifies the user.

Creating the UserRegistrationSystem Application

You will be creating UserRegistrationSystem by generating a Spring Boot application using Spring Initializr, as shown in Figure 2-1. Select Web, JPA, and H2 as dependencies. By default, the Spring Boot application runs on port 8080.

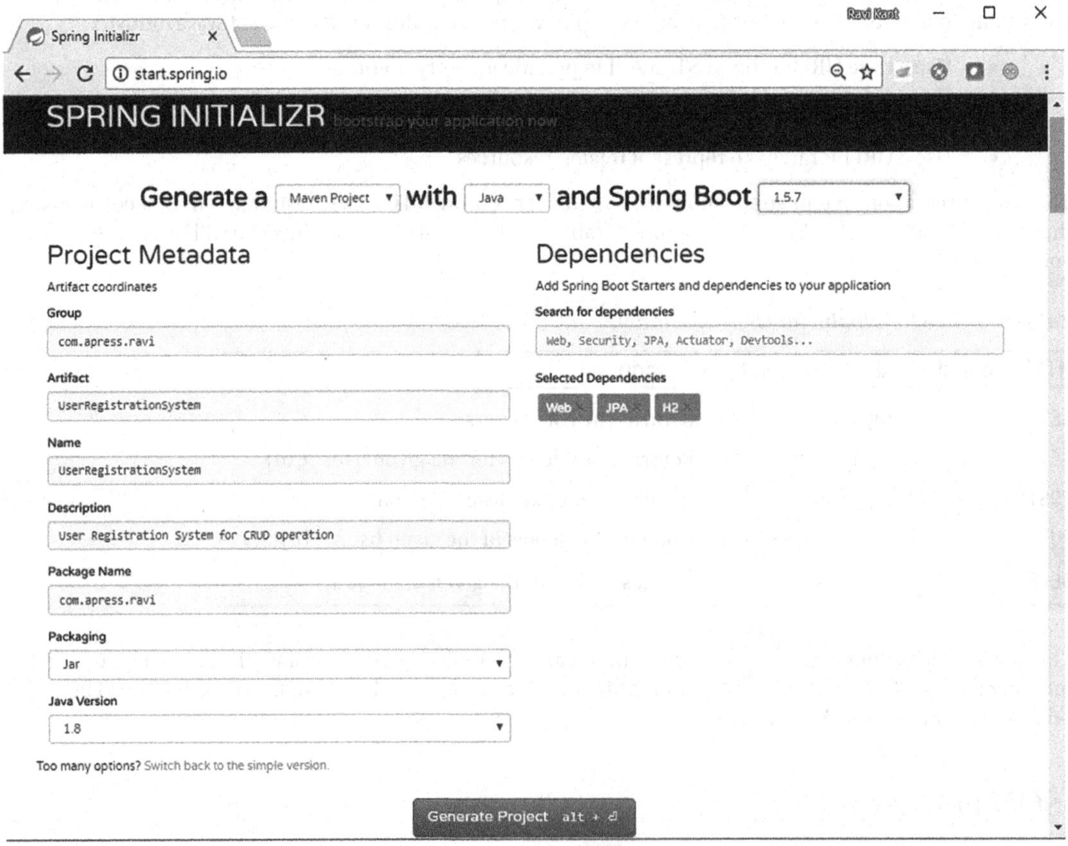

Figure 2-1. *Creating UserRegistrationSystem using Spring Initializr*

Embedded Database: H2

H2 is an open source lightweight relational database management system written in Java. The H2 database can be easily embedded in any Java-based application and can be easily configured to run as an in-memory database. The H2 database cannot be used for production development because the data will not persist on the disk. That's why this database is mostly used for development and testing. The H2 database supports SQL and the JDBC API and has strong security features.

In the UserRegistrationSystem application, you will be using H2 to persist your data. To use H2 in a Spring Boot application, you need to include a build dependency in the `pom.xml` file.

While using H2 as an in-memory database, you do not need to provide any database connection URLs or username and password. The starting and stopping of the database during deployment and application shutdown will be taken care by Spring Boot. Listing 2-2 shows the dependency information for H2 in UserRegistrationSystem's `pom.xml` file.

Listing 2-2. H2 Dependency in pom.xml

```
<dependency>
        <groupId>com.h2database</groupId>
        <artifactId>h2</artifactId>
        <scope>runtime</scope>
</dependency>
```

Domain Implementation: Users

Figure 2-2 shows the UML class diagram representing the `Users` domain object in the UserRegistrationSystem application.

Users
- id : Long - name: String - address: String - email: String
+ getId(): Long + setId(Long id) + getName(): String + setName(String name) + getAddress(): String + setAddress(String address) + getEmail(): String + setEmail(String email)

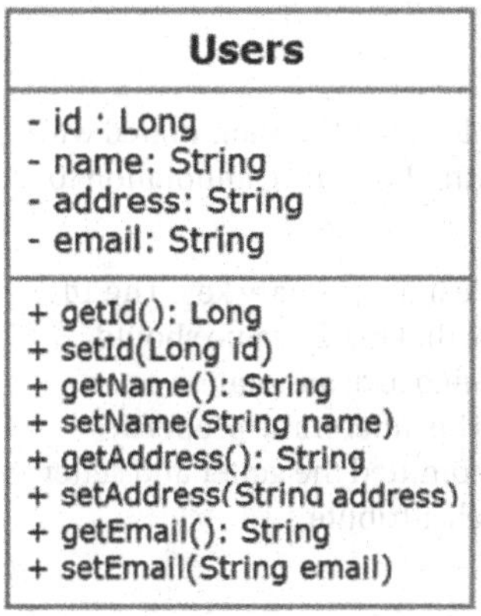

Figure 2-2. *Users domain object*

In the UserRegistrationSystem project, you will create a data transfer object (DTO) class called `UserDTO` corresponding to the `Users` domain's `Object` inside a subpackage called `com.apress.ravi.dto` under the `src/main/java` folder.

The DTO object contains just data and access modifiers and no logic; it is used to transfer data between different layers of the application when there is a separation of concerns. You can annotate this class with Java Persistence API (JPA) annotations, which allows the `Users` class to be easily persisted and retrieved using the JPA technology. A formal overview of JPA is beyond the scope of this book. Listing 2-3 gives the implementation of the `UserDTO` entity class.

33

Listing 2-3. UsersDTO Entity Class

```
package com.apress.ravi.dto;

import javax.persistence.Column;
import javax.persistence.Entity;
import javax.persistence.GeneratedValue;
import javax.persistence.Id;

@Entity
@Table(name="Users")
public class UserDTO {

        @Id
        @GeneratedValue
        @Column(name = "USER_ID")
        private Long id;

        @Column(name = "NAME")
        private String name;

        @Column(name = "ADDRESS")
        private String address;

        @Column(name = "EMAIL")
        private String email;

        // Getters and Setters methods
}
```

Here the UserDTO class has four attributes, named id, name, address, and email. UserDTO is annotated with the @Entity annotation to make it a JPA entity. This entity class is annotated with the @Table annotation to define the table name as Users.

The UserDTO's id property has been annotated with the @Id annotation to make it the primary key. The id attribute has been annotated with the @GeneratedValue annotation to indicate that the id value should be generated automatically. The id attribute also has been annotated with the @Column annotation to specify the details of the column to which a field or property will be mapped. The other three properties (name, address, and email) are annotated with the @Column annotation. I have omitted the getter and setter methods here, but in the actual code there should be a getter and setter for each attribute.

The next step is to provide the repository or DAO implementation.

Repository Implementation: UserJpaRepository

Repositories or DAOs abstract and encapsulate all access to the data source. The repository includes an interface that manages the connection with the data source and provides a set of methods for retrieving, manipulating, deleting, and persisting data. It is good practice to have one repository per domain object.

With the goal of eliminating the need to write any repository implementations, the Spring Data project provided the JpaRepository interface that automatically generates its implementation at runtime. Listing 2-4 shows the dependency information that needs to be in the Maven pom.xml to support JpaRepository.

Listing 2-4. JPA Dependency in pom.xml

```
<dependency>
        <groupId>org.springframework.boot</groupId>
        <artifactId>spring-boot-starter-data-jpa</artifactId>
</dependency>
```

You will be creating a repository interface by extending the Spring Data JPA subproject's `org.springframework.data.jpa.repository.JpaRepository` interface to persist the `UserDTO` domain object into a relational database.

You begin the repository implementation by creating the `com.apress.ravi.repository` package under the `src/main/java` folder inside the UserRegistrationSystem application. Also, you can create a `UserJpaRepository` interface, as shown in Listing 2-5.

Listing 2-5. com.apress.ravi.repository.UserJpaRepository.java Interface

```
package com.apress.ravi.repository;

import org.springframework.data.jpa.repository.JpaRepository;
import org.springframework.stereotype.Repository;

import com.apress.ravi.dto.UsersDTO;

@Repository
public interface UserJpaRepository extends JpaRepository<UsersDTO, Long> {

        UsersDTO findByName(String name);
}
```

As shown in Listing 2-5, the `UserJpaRepository` interface extends Spring Data's `JpaRepository`, which takes the type of domain object that it can manipulate and the type of `UserDTO` domain object's identifier field, `UserDTO` and `Long`, as its generic parameters, `T` and `ID`. `UserJpaRepository` inherits all of `JpaRepository`'s CRUD methods for working with `UserDTO` persistence.

Spring Data JPA allows developers to define other query methods just by declaring their method signature. As shown in the previous code, you define a custom finder method called `findByName`, which basically creates a JPA query of the form `select u from UserDTO u`, where `u.name` equals `:name"`.

The benefit of Spring Data JPA is that developers do not have to write implementations of the repository interface. Spring Data JPA creates an implementation at runtime when you run the application. Now, let's create the REST controller class and implement the REST endpoints.

Build a RESTful API

Before you start implementing the RESTful API, you need to understand some basic Spring elements that will be used to implement the RESTful API in Spring.

- `@RestController`: This is a stereotype annotation that itself is annotated with `@Controller` and `@ResponseBody`, which eliminates the need of annotating each method with `@ResponseBody`. This annotation is used to define an API endpoint. This annotation lets Spring render the result back to the caller. To build RESTful web services in Spring, create a controller class using the `@RestController` annotation to handle the HTTP request.

```
@Target(value=TYPE)
@Retention(value=RUNTIME)
@Documented
@Controller
@ResponseBody
public @interface RestController
```

- @RequestMapping: This annotation is used to provide routing information. The HTTP request in Spring is mapped to the corresponding handler method. This annotation can be applied to the class level to map the HTTP request to the controller class or can be applied to the method level to map the HTTP request to the controller handler method.

```
@Target(value={METHOD,TYPE})
@Retention(value=RUNTIME)
@Documented
public @interface RequestMapping
```

- ResponseEntity: This class extends HttpEntity and is used in the controller method to add the HTTP status to the response. It can contain HTTP status codes, headers, and the body.

```
public class ResponseEntity<T>
extends HttpEntity<T>
```

- @RequestBody: This annotation is used to bind the method parameter to the body of the incoming HTTP request. Spring will use an HttpMessageConverter to convert the body of the web request into a domain object depending on the content type of the request. The @valid annotation can be applied to perform automatic validation, which is optional.

```
@Target(value=PARAMETER)
@Retention(value=RUNTIME)
@Documented
public @interface RequestBody
```

- @ResponseBody: This annotation is used to bind the return value from the annotated method to the outgoing HTTP response body. Spring will use an HttpMessageConverter to convert the return value to the HTTP response body (typically to return data formats such as JSON or XML), depending on the content type of the request HTTP header.

```
@Target(value={TYPE,METHOD})
@Retention(value=RUNTIME)
@Documented
public @interface ResponseBody
```

- @PathVariable: This annotation is used to bind a method parameter to a URI template variable (the one in {}).

```
@Target(value=PARAMETER)
@Retention(value=RUNTIME)
```

```
@Documented
public @interface PathVariable
```

- MediaType: This is a subclass of MimeType. While using the @RequestMapping
  annotation, you can also specify the MediaType to be produced or consumed by the
  controller method.

```
public class MediaType
extends MimeType
implements Serializable
```

Create a RESTful Controller: UserRegistrationRestController

You will be creating a Spring MVC controller and implementing REST API endpoints. Let's create the
UserRegistrationRestController class within the com.apress.ravi.Rest package under the src/main/
java folder. This controller class provides all the necessary endpoints to retrieve and manipulate users.
Listing 2-6 shows the necessary code changes for the UserRegistrationRestController class.

Listing 2-6. UserRegistrationRestController Class

```
package com.apress.ravi.Rest;

import org.slf4j.Logger;
import org.slf4j.LoggerFactory;
import org.springframework.beans.factory.annotation.Autowired;
import org.springframework.web.bind.annotation.RequestMapping;
import org.springframework.web.bind.annotation.RestController;

import com.apress.ravi.repository.UserJpaRepository;

@RestController
@RequestMapping("/api/user")
public class UserRegistrationRestController {
        public static final Logger logger =
                LoggerFactory.getLogger(UserRegistrationRestController.class);

        private UserJpaRepository userJpaRepository;

        @Autowired
        public void setUserJpaRepository(UserJpaRepository userJpaRepository) {
                this.userJpaRepository = userJpaRepository;
        }
}
```

In Listing 2-6, you annotated the UserRegistrationRestController class with the @RestController
annotation and defined a new @RequestMapping to map the URI /api/user to the entire class, which means
the HTTP request received on the /api/user URI is attended by the UserRegistrationRestController
class. You have used the @Autowired annotation to autowireUserJpaRepository to the RESTful controller.

Let's define different endpoints in the controller class to access and manipulate UserDTO. You will be using the new annotations @GetMapping, @PostMapping, @PutMapping, and @DeleteMapping instead of the standard @RequestMapping, which have been available since Spring MVC 4.3 and are a standard way of defining REST endpoints. These new annotations act as a wrapper to @RequestMapping, simplifying mappings for common HTTP methods.

@GetMapping: Retrieve All Users

This is a composed annotation that is a shortcut for @RequestMapping(value="/", method = RequestMethod.GET). The GET request on the /api/user/ endpoint returns the list of users available in the UserRegistrationSystem application. Listing 2-7 shows the necessary code for implementing this functionality.

Listing 2-7. GET Verb Implementation to Retrieve All Users

```
@GetMapping("/")
public ResponseEntity<List<UsersDTO>> listAllUsers() {
        List<UsersDTO> users = userJpaRepository.findAll();
        return new ResponseEntity<List<UsersDTO>>(users, HttpStatus.OK);
}
```

The listAllUsers method returns ResponseEntity containing the HTTP response. This method reads all of the users using UserJpaRepository. You then created an instance of ResponseEntity by calling its constructor, which takes two arguments: UserDTO is data that became part of the response body, and the HttpStatus.OK status value is data that became the response status code.

Let's test the first endpoint by running the UserRegistrationSystem application as a Spring Boot application from STS and launching the Postman app. Enter the URL http://localhost:8080/api/user/ and hit Send, as shown in Figure 2-3.

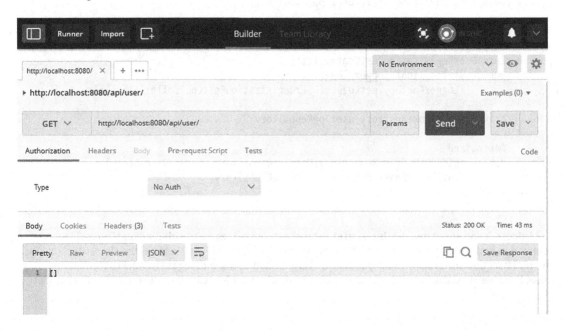

Figure 2-3. *GET verb implementation to retrieve all users*

Because there are no users created yet, this results in an empty collection. So, the next task is to add a user to UserRegistrationSystem by implementing the POST verb functionality.

@PostMapping: Create a New User

The @PostMapping annotation is a composed annotation that is a shortcut for @RequestMapping(value="/", method=RequestMethod.POST). The POST request on the /api/user/ endpoint creates a new user using the enclosed body of the request. Listing 2-8 shows the necessary code for implementing the POST verb functionality.

Listing 2-8. POST Verb Implementation to Create a New User

```
@PostMapping(value = "/", consumes = MediaType.APPLICATION_JSON_VALUE)
public ResponseEntity<UsersDTO> createUser(@RequestBody final UsersDTO user) {
        userJpaRepository.save(user);
        return new ResponseEntity<UsersDTO>(user, HttpStatus.CREATED);
}
```

The createUser method takes a parameter of type UsersDTO annotated with the @RequestBody annotation, which requests Spring to convert the entire request body to an instance of UserDTO.

You have configured content negotiation using consumes = MediaType.APPLICATION_JSON_VALUE, which indicates this method will accept only JSON data from the request body. The produces and consumes attributes are used to narrow the mapping types. You can eliminate this because @RequestBody uses HttpMessageConverters to determine the right converter to use and to convert the body of the HTTP request to domain objects. The message converters in Spring BOOT support JSON and XML resource representations.

Inside the method, you delegated the UserDTO persistence to userJpaRepository's save method. Then you created a new ResponseEntity with the created user (UserDTO) and HTTP status HttpStatus.CREATED (201) and returned it.

To test this newly added endpoint, start the UserRegistrationSystem application. If the UserRegistrationSystem application is already running, then you need to terminate the process and restart it. Launch Postman and select the request type as POST. Click Body and select raw; then from the drop-down, select JSON (application/json) as the Content-Type header. Enter some information and hit Send. Listing 2-9 shows the JSON used in the body.

Listing 2-9. JSON Used in the Body to Create a New User

```
{
        "name":"Ravi Kant Soni",
        "address":"Lashkariganj, Sasaram, Rohtas, Bihar, pin-821115",
        "email":"ravikantsoni.author@gmail.com"
}
```

On completion of the request, you will see a 201 Created message, as shown in Figure 2-4.

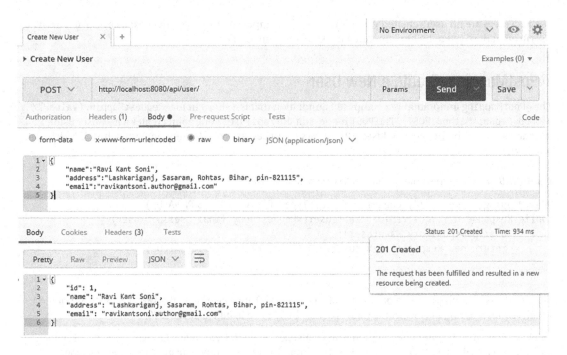

Figure 2-4. *POST verb implementation to create a new user*

@GetMapping ("/ {id}"): Retrieve an Individual User

The next step is to implement an endpoint to access an individual user. Listing 2-10 shows the necessary code.

Listing 2-10. GET Verb Implementation to Retrieve Individual User

```
@GetMapping("/{id}")
public ResponseEntity<UsersDTO> getUserById(@PathVariable("id") final Long id) {
        UsersDTO user = userJpaRepository.findById(id);
        return new ResponseEntity<UsersDTO>(user, HttpStatus.OK);
}
```

As shown in Listing 2-10, you have annotated the getUserById method with the @GetMapping("/{id}") annotation. The placeholder {id} in the URI along with the @PathVariable annotation allows Spring to extract the id parameter value. Inside the method, you have used UserJpaRepository's findById method to read the UserDTO object and pass it as part of a ResponseEntity along with the HTTP status HttpStatus.OK (200).

To test this functionality, launch Postman and restart the UserRegistrationSystem application. Enter the URL http://localhost:8080/api/user/1 and hit Send, as shown in Figure 2-5.

Figure 2-5. Retrieving individual user

Similarly, you can implement an endpoint to perform the update and delete functionality.

@PutMapping: Update a User

This annotation is a composed annotation that is a shortcut for @RequestMapping(method = RequestMethod.PUT). It requests that the enclosed entity be considered as a modified version of an existing resource at the request URI. Listing 2-11 shows the necessary code.

Listing 2-11. PUT Verb Implementation to Update a User

```
@PutMapping(value = "/{id}", consumes = MediaType.APPLICATION_JSON_VALUE)
public ResponseEntity<UsersDTO> updateUser(
                @PathVariable("id") final Long id, @RequestBody UsersDTO user) {

        // fetch user based on id and set it to currentUser object of type UserDTO
        UsersDTO currentUser = userJpaRepository.findById(id);

        // update currentUser object data  with user object data
        currentUser.setName(user.getName());
        currentUser.setAddress(user.getAddress());
        currentUser.setEmail(user.getEmail());

        // save currentUser obejct
        userJpaRepository.saveAndFlush(currentUser);

        //return ResponseEntity object
        return new ResponseEntity<UsersDTO>(currentUser, HttpStatus.OK);
}
```

In Listing 2-11, you retrieved the existing UserDTO object as currentUser using UserJpaRepository's findById method by passing the argument as id from pathvariable. Then you updated the currentUser property data from the user's information in requestbody.

You also called UserJpaRepository's saveAndFlush method by passing currentUser, which saves UserDTO and flushes the changes instantly. Finally, you returned ResponseEntity with currentUser as the response body and HttpStatus.OK as the HTTP status.

Let's test this endpoint by launching Postman and restarting the application, as shown in Figure 2-6.

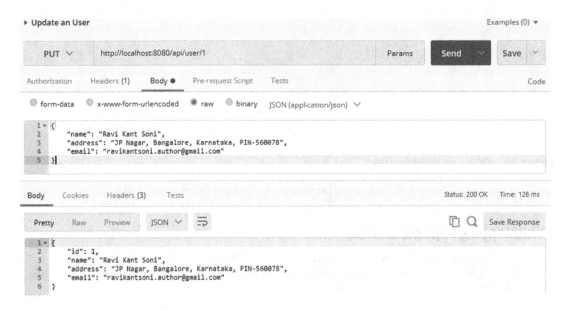

Figure 2-6. *PUT verb implementation to update a user*

Now let's implement the delete functionality to delete an existing user from the UserRegistrationSystem application.

@DeleteMapping: Delete a User

This is a composed annotation that is a shortcut for @RequestMapping(method = RequestMethod.DELETE). It requests that the application deletes resources identified by Request-URI. Listing 2-12 shows the necessary code for implementing this functionality.

Listing 2-12. DELETE Verb Implementation to Delete a User

```
@DeleteMapping("/{id}")
public ResponseEntity<UsersDTO> deleteUser(@PathVariable("id") final Long id) {
        userJpaRepository.delete(id);
        return new ResponseEntity<UsersDTO>(HttpStatus.NO_CONTENT);
}
```

In Listing 2-12, the inside method you called `UserJpaRepository`'s delete method by passing the argument id from `pathvariable`. And, then you returned `ResponseEntity` with an HTTP status of `HttpStatus.NO_CONTENT (204)`.

Restart the UserRegistrationSystem application and launch Postman to test this functionality, as shown in Figure 2-7.

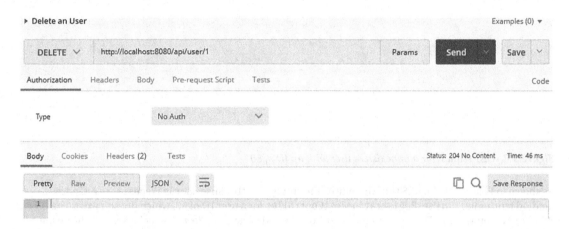

Figure 2-7. *DELETE verb implementation to delete a user*

Up to now you learned about how to implement a RESTful API to perform CRUD operations. Now you will learn about error handling in a RESTful API.

Handle Errors in a RESTful API

Although a developer takes care of handling error, it is important to design error responses in a suitable format that allows a client who consumes a RESTful API to understand the issues and help by using the API correctly. Error handling is one of the most important concerns of RESTful API development. In the real world, a RESTful API is being consumed in various scenarios, and it is difficult to predict everything about the scenario in which the API is being consumed.

UserRegistrationSystem Error Handling

Consider a scenario in the UserRegistrationSystem application where the client tries to fetch user information that doesn't exist in the system. Figure 2-8 shows the Postman `GET` request for a nonexistent user with an ID of 50.

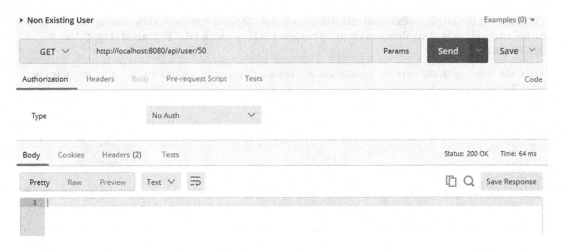

Figure 2-8. *GET request for a nonexistent user with an ID of 50*

As shown in Figure 2-8, the RESTful API returns the empty body because UserJpaRepository's findOne method returns null to UserRegistrationRestController for a user ID of 50, which doesn't exist. The RESTful API returns the HTTP status code as 200 OK, instead of status code 404, which should indicate the requested user doesn't exist.

To achieve this behavior, you will validate the user id attribute in com.apress.ravi.Rest. UserRegistrationRestController's getUserById method. For a nonexistent user, return ResponseEntity containing CustomErrorType and status code HttpStatus.NOT_FOUND (404). Listing 2-13 shows the necessary code update for handling errors.

Listing 2-13. Error Handing for Nonexistent User

```
@GetMapping("/{id}")
public ResponseEntity<UsersDTO> getUserById(@PathVariable("id") final Long id) {
        UsersDTO user = userJpaRepository.findById(id);
        if (user == null) {
                return new ResponseEntity<UsersDTO>(
                        new CustomErrorType("User with id "
                        + id + " not found"), HttpStatus.NOT_FOUND);
        }
        return new ResponseEntity<UsersDTO>(user, HttpStatus.OK);
}
```

In Listing 2-13, you have created an instance of the CustomErrorType class by passing a custom error message ("User with id 50 not found") in its constructor.

Custom Error Response

Now let's create the CustomErrorType class in the com.apress.ravi.Exception package under src/main/java. Listing 2-14 shows the necessary code implementation for the CustomErrorType class.

Listing 2-14. CustomErrorType Class

```
package com.apress.ravi.Exception;

import com.apress.ravi.dto.UsersDTO;

public class CustomErrorType extends UsersDTO {

private String errorMessage;

    public CustomErrorType(final String errorMessage){
        this.errorMessage = errorMessage;
    }

@Override
    public String getErrorMessage() {
        return errorMessage;
    }
}
```

In Listing 2-14, the CustomErrorType class declared errorMessage as a member variable with its corresponding getter method. This errorMessage is getting initialized inside the constructor of this class.

With this modification in the UserRegistrationSystem application, restart the application and launch Postman to send a GET request for the user with an ID of 50. The UserRegistrationRestController result with the right status code and error message is shown in Figure 2-9.

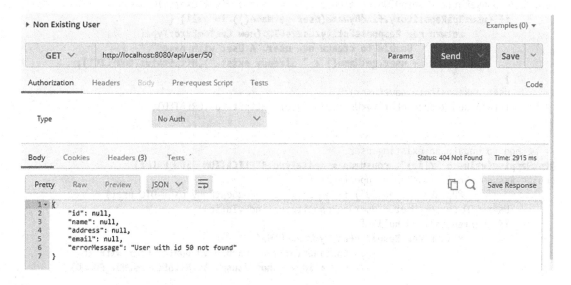

Figure 2-9. *Error message and status code for nonexistent user*

The same user ID verification needs to be performed for other methods that are involved in CRUD operations with HTTP methods such as GET, PUT, and DELETE in the UserRegistrationSystem application to return the right status code and message. Listing 2-15 shows the updated UserRegistrationRestController class with the modified listAllUsers, getUserById, createUser, updateUser, and deleteUser methods.

Listing 2-15. Updated UserRegistrationRestController Class

```java
// method to get list of users
@GetMapping("/")
public ResponseEntity<List<UsersDTO>> listAllUsers() {
        List<UsersDTO> users = userJpaRepository.findAll();
        if (users.isEmpty()) {
                return new ResponseEntity<List<UsersDTO>>(HttpStatus.NO_CONTENT);
        }
        return new ResponseEntity<List<UsersDTO>>(users, HttpStatus.OK);
}


// method to get user by id
@GetMapping("/{id}")
public ResponseEntity<UsersDTO> getUserById(@PathVariable("id") final Long id) {
        UsersDTO user = userJpaRepository.findById(id);
        if (user == null) {
                return new ResponseEntity<UsersDTO>(
                                new CustomErrorType("User with id "
                                + id + " not found"), HttpStatus.NOT_FOUND);
        }
        return new ResponseEntity<UsersDTO>(user, HttpStatus.OK);
}


// method to create an user
@PostMapping(value = "/", consumes = MediaType.APPLICATION_JSON_VALUE)
public ResponseEntity<UsersDTO> createUser(@RequestBody final UsersDTO user) {
        if (userJpaRepository.findByName(user.getName()) != null) {
                return new ResponseEntity<UsersDTO>(new CustomErrorType(
                                "Unable to create new user. A User with name "
                                + user.getName() + " already exist."),HttpStatus.CONFLICT);
        }
        userJpaRepository.save(user);
        return new ResponseEntity<UsersDTO>(user, HttpStatus.CREATED);
}


// method to update an existing user
@PutMapping(value = "/{id}", consumes = MediaType.APPLICATION_JSON_VALUE)
public ResponseEntity<UsersDTO> updateUser(
                        @PathVariable("id") final Long id, @RequestBody UsersDTO user) {
        UsersDTO currentUser = userJpaRepository.findById(id);
        if (currentUser == null) {
                return new ResponseEntity<UsersDTO>(
                                        new CustomErrorType("Unable to upate. User with id "
                                                + id + " not found."), HttpStatus.NOT_FOUND);
        }
```

```
                currentUser.setName(user.getName());
                currentUser.setAddress(user.getAddress());
                currentUser.setEmail(user.getEmail());
                userJpaRepository.saveAndFlush(currentUser);
                return new ResponseEntity<UsersDTO>(currentUser, HttpStatus.OK);
        }

        // delete an existing user
        @DeleteMapping("/{id}")
        public ResponseEntity<UsersDTO> deleteUser(@PathVariable("id") final Long id) {
                UsersDTO user = userJpaRepository.findById(id);
                if (user == null) {
                        return new ResponseEntity<UsersDTO>(
                                        new CustomErrorType("Unable to delete. User with id "
                                                + id + " not found."), HttpStatus.NOT_FOUND);
                }
                userJpaRepository.delete(id);
                return new ResponseEntity<UsersDTO>(
                                        new CustomErrorType("Deleted User with id "
                                                + id + "."), HttpStatus.NO_CONTENT);
        }
```

Validating Request Body

When it is required to validate the request body containing JSON data for some complex object, you have to do a bit more. Consider a scenario where a client makes a new user creation request with missing data in the request body, such as the request body doesn't include an address.

Spring MVC supports input validation using JSR-303 Bean Validation constraints.

Adding the Bean Validation Annotations

Listing 2-16 shows the update in the UsersDTO entity class. You annotate your UsersDTO object properties with validation constraints such as @NotNull and @Email. You can use Hibernate Validator, which is a popular JSR 303 and JSR 349 implementation framework.

Listing 2-16. UsersDTO Class Annotated with JSR 303 Annotations

```
package com.apress.ravi.dto;

import javax.persistence.Column;
import javax.persistence.Entity;
import javax.persistence.GeneratedValue;
import javax.persistence.Id;

import org.hibernate.validator.constraints.Email;
import org.hibernate.validator.constraints.Length;
import org.hibernate.validator.constraints.NotEmpty;
```

```
@Entity
public class UsersDTO {

        @Id
        @GeneratedValue
        @Column(name = "USER_ID")
        private Long id;

        @NotEmpty
        @Length(max = 50)
        @Column(name = "NAME")
        private String name;

        @NotEmpty
        @Length(max = 150)
        @Column(name = "ADDRESS")
        private String address;

        @Email
        @NotEmpty
        @Length(max = 80)
        @Column(name = "EMAIL")
        private String email;

        // Getter & Setter method

}
```

As shown in Listing 2-16, you have annotated the UsersDTO class to add input validation capabilities to the UserRegistrationSystem application. Table 2-4 shows some of the validation constraints available with the Bean Validation API.

Table 2-4. *Validation Constraints Available with the Bean Validation API*

Constraint	Description
NotNull	The annotated member variable must not be null.
NotEmpty	The annotated member variable (string, collection, map, or array) is not null or empty.
Size	The annotated member variable (string, collection, map, or array) size must be between the specified boundaries (included).
Length	This performs an update operation.
Email	The annotated member variable (string) has to be a well-formed valid e-mail address.
Min	The annotated member variable (BigDecimal, BigInteger, Byte, Short, int, long, and their wrapper classes) must be a number whose value must be higher or equal to the specified minimum.
Max	The annotated member variable (BigDecimal, BigInteger, Byte, Short, int, long, and their wrapper class) must be a number whose value must be lower or equal to the specified minimum.

Because you want to make sure that each user has name, address, and e-mail, you have annotated these fields with the @NotEmpty annotation, which ensures that the input string is not null and its length is greater than zero. You have also annotated these fields with the @Length and a max value to ensure that the String length should exceed this max length value. The e-mail field is annotated with the @Email annotation to validate the input string with a valid e-mail address.

The next step is to add the @Valid annotation to the createUser method's UsersDTO parameter in the UserRegistrationRestController class.

@Valid on @RequestBody in UserRegistrationRestController Method Arguments

Add the @Valid annotation to the createUser method's UsersDTO parameter in the UserRegistrationRestController endpoint, as shown in Listing 2-17.

Listing 2-17. UserRegistrationRestController Annotated with @Valid Annotations

```
@PostMapping(value = "/", consumes = MediaType.APPLICATION_JSON_VALUE)
public ResponseEntity<UsersDTO> createUser(
                @Valid @RequestBody final UsersDTO user) {
        logger.info("Creating User : {}", user);
        if (userJpaRepository.findByName(user.getName()) != null) {
        logger.error("Unable to create. A User with name {} already exist",
                            user.getName());
                return new ResponseEntity<UsersDTO>(
                    new CustomErrorType(
                        "Unable to create new user. A User with name "
                        + user.getName() + " already exist."),
                        HttpStatus.CONFLICT);
        }
        userJpaRepository.save(user);
        return new ResponseEntity<UsersDTO>(user, HttpStatus.CREATED);
}
```

As shown in Listing 2-17, the @Valid annotation will instruct Spring to perform request data validation after binding incoming POST parameters with an object.

The @RequestBody method argument can be annotated with @Valid to invoke automatic validation similar to the support for @ModelAttribute method arguments. A resulting MethodArgumentNotValidException is handled in the DefaultHandlerExceptionResolver and results in a 400 response code.

■ **Source**   See http://docs.spring.io/spring/docs/3.2.18.RELEASE/spring-framework-reference/htmlsingle/#new-in-3.1-mvc-valid-requestbody.

By using the @Valid annotation, Spring delegates the validation to a registered validator. On running the UserRegistrationSystem application and sending a Postman request with a missing address, as shown in Figure 2-10, the error code HTTP status 400, Bad Request, indicates operation the failed.

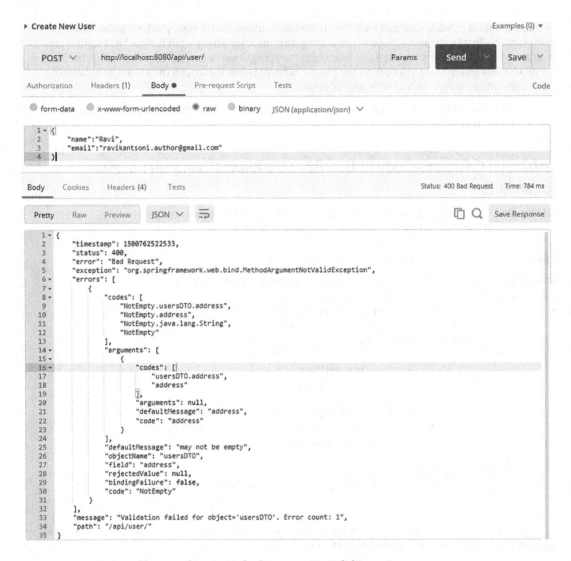

Figure 2-10. *Missing address resulting in MethodArgumentNotValidException*

On repeating the Postman request with a missing question, as you did in Figure 5-7, you will see the operation fail with the following information, as shown in Figure 5-8:

- *Status*: 400

- *Error*: Bad request

- *Exception*: org.springframework.web.bind.MethodArgumentNotValidException

From this error response, you can understand that Spring MVC validated the input data and threw a MethodArgumentNotValidException exception when it did not find the required address field.

Even though the error message returned from Spring Boot is helpful, it's not that informative to the client consuming the RESTful API. So, you should present an error message that's more informative, as shown here in JSON format:

```
{
        "error_title" : "",
        "error_status" : "",
        "error_detail" : "",
        "error_timestamp" : "",
        "error_path" : "",
        "error_developerMessage"": "",
        "errors": {
                "field1" : [ {
                        "field" : ""
                        "message" : ""
                        "type" : ""
                },
                "field2" : [ {
                        "field" : ""
                        "message" : ""
                        "type" : ""
                }
        }
}
```

To represent this JSON format for an error message, it is required that you intercept MethodArgumentNotValidException and return an appropriate error message. While designing the UserRegistrationSystem error response, you came up with error object that can contain an unordered collection of key-value error instances, where key contains field name, and values contains a field's error information containing field, message, and type, as shown in the previous JSON data.

Keeping the previous JSON error message design in mind, let's create classes to return an instance containing an appropriate error message in JSON format.

ValidationError and Updated ErrorDetail Classes

To add the previous validation error feature in the UserRegistrationSystem application, you need to create two classes.

- com.apress.ravi.Exception.FieldValidationError
- com.apress.ravi.Exception.FieldValidationErrorDetails

Listing 2-18 shows the FieldValidationError class.

Listing 2-18. FieldValidationError Class

```
import java.awt.TrayIcon.MessageType;

public class FieldValidationError {

        private String filed;
        private String message;
```

```
        private MessageType type;

        // Getter & Setter

}
```

The FieldValidationError class has three properties: a field (String), a message (String), and the message type (MessageType).

MessageType is an enumeration containing the possible message types, as shown in Listing 2-19.

Listing 2-19. Enumeration MessageType

```
public enum MessageType {

        SUCCESS, INFO, WARNING, ERROR

}
```

The FieldValidationErrorDetails class instance will be created to generate an error response format as an expected error JSON format, as shown in Listing 2-20.

Listing 2-20. FieldValidationErrorDetails Class

```
package com.apress.ravi.Exception;

import java.util.HashMap;
import java.util.List;
import java.util.Map;

public class FieldValidationErrorDetails {

        private String error_title;
        private int error_status;
        private String error_detail;
        private long error_timeStamp;
        private String error_path;
        private String error_developer_Message;
        private Map<String, List<FieldValidationError>> errors =
                        new HashMap<String, List<FieldValidationError>>();

        // Getter & Setter

}
```

The errors field in the FieldValidationErrorDetails class is defined as a Map that accepts String instances as keys and a list of FieldValidationError instances as values.

The next step is to create a class to intercept and process the MethodArgumentNotValidException exception.

Handling Exceptions Using the @ControllerAdvice Annotation

The @ControllerAdvice annotation is used to define a global exception handler for an exception handler method annotated using the @ExceptionHandler annotation.

A class annotated with the @ControllerAdvice annotation will be applicable to all controllers in the application. So, any exception thrown by any controller class in that application will be handled by this annotated class having a method annotated with the @ExceptionHandler annotation. This method will be executed only if any controller classes throw an exception matching the configured Exception class.

So, let's create the controller advice class RestValidationHandler inside the com.apress.ravi.Exception package under the src/main/java folder, which intercepts the exception, as shown in Listing 2-21.

Listing 2-21. Controller Advice Class to handleValidationError

```
package com.apress.ravi.Exception;

import java.awt.TrayIcon.MessageType;
import java.util.ArrayList;
import java.util.Date;
import java.util.List;

import javax.servlet.http.HttpServletRequest;

import org.springframework.http.HttpStatus;
import org.springframework.http.ResponseEntity;
import org.springframework.validation.BindingResult;
import org.springframework.validation.FieldError;
import org.springframework.web.bind.MethodArgumentNotValidException;
import org.springframework.web.bind.annotation.ControllerAdvice;
import org.springframework.web.bind.annotation.ExceptionHandler;
import org.springframework.web.bind.annotation.ResponseStatus;

@ControllerAdvice
public class RestValidationHandler {

        // method to handle validation error
        @ExceptionHandler(MethodArgumentNotValidException.class)
        @ResponseStatus(HttpStatus.BAD_REQUEST)
        public ResponseEntity<FieldValidationErrorDetails> handleValidationError(
                        MethodArgumentNotValidException mNotValidException,
                        HttpServletRequest request) {

                FieldValidationErrorDetails fErrorDetails =
                                        new FieldValidationErrorDetails();

                fErrorDetails.setError_timeStamp(new Date().getTime());
                fErrorDetails.setError_status(HttpStatus.BAD_REQUEST.value());
                fErrorDetails.setError_title("Field Validation Error");
                fErrorDetails.setError_detail("Inut Field Validation Failed");
                fErrorDetails.setError_developer_Message(
                                        mNotValidException.getClass().getName());
                fErrorDetails.setError_path(request.getRequestURI());
```

```
            BindingResult result = mNotValidException.getBindingResult();
            List<FieldError> fieldErrors = result.getFieldErrors();

            for (FieldError error : fieldErrors) {
                    FieldValidationError fError = processFieldError(error);
                    List<FieldValidationError> fValidationErrorsList =
                            fErrorDetails.getErrors().get(error.getField());
                    if (fValidationErrorsList == null) {
                            fValidationErrorsList =
                                    new ArrayList<FieldValidationError>();
                    }
                    fValidationErrorsList.add(fError);
                    fErrorDetails.getErrors().put(
                                    error.getField(), fValidationErrorsList);
            }
            return new ResponseEntity<FieldValidationErrorDetails>(
                            fErrorDetails, HttpStatus.BAD_REQUEST);
    }

    // method to process field error
    private FieldValidationError processFieldError(final FieldError error) {
            FieldValidationError fieldValidationError =
                                            new FieldValidationError();
            if (error != null) {
                    fieldValidationError.setFiled(error.getField());
                    fieldValidationError.setType(MessageType.ERROR);
                    fieldValidationError.setMessage(error.getDefaultMessage());
            }
            return fieldValidationError;
    }
}
```

As shown in Listing 2-21, RestValidationHandler is annotated with the @ControllerAdvice annotation from the org.springframework.web.bind.annotation package. This class defines a global exception handler method called handleValidationError with the @ExceptionHandler(MethodArgumentNotValidExc eption.class) annotation to intercept an exception of type MethodArgumentNotValidException thrown by any controller class from the UserRegistrationSystem application.

The implementation of the handlerValidationError method begins by creating an instance of FieldValidationErrorDetails and populating it with appropriate information by calling the setter method for different fields. Then you use the passed-in exception parameter mNotValidException to obtain a field errors list and loop through the list to get error information. You then create an instance of FieldValidationError for each field error and populate it with code and error information.

With this implementation, let's restart the UserRegistrationSystem application and submit the user with a missing address from Postman. This missing POST data request with a missing address will result in a status code of 400 with a custom error response, as shown in Figure 2-11.

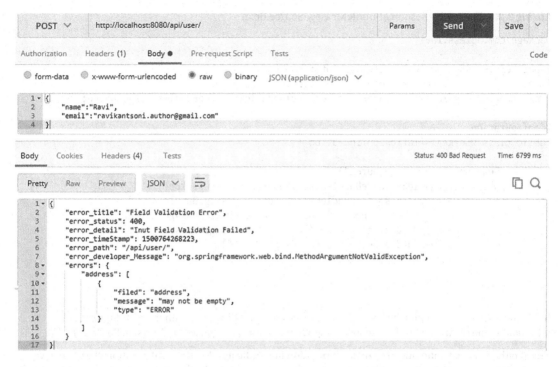

Figure 2-11. *Custom error message for creating a user with a missing address result*

Externalizing Error Messages

Up to now you have made good progress with input data validation, and the client is able to receive a descriptive error message that lets the client troubleshoot issues and recover from those errors while consuming the API.

Even though the error message that you saw in the previous section is descriptive, an API developer can make it more descriptive by pulling this message from the external messages.properties file. This properties file approach allows an API developer to easily swap the message without making any changes in code. It also supports internationalization/localization.

The next step is to read the properties file so that properties from this file can be used during the ValidationError instance creation. To achieve that feature, you have to configure ReloadableResourceBundleMessageSource in your application configuration class.

Create ReloadableResourceBundleMessageSource Bean: messageSource

Let's create a ReloadableResourceBundleMessageSource bean in the UserRegistrationConfiguration class inside the com.apress.ravi package under the src/main/java folder. Listing 2-22 shows the necessary code changes.

Listing 2-22. ReloadableResourceBundleMessageSource Bean

```
package com.apress.ravi;

import org.springframework.context.annotation.Bean;
import org.springframework.context.annotation.Configuration;
import org.springframework.context.support.ReloadableResourceBundleMessageSource;

@Configuration
public class UserRegistrationConfiguration {

        @Bean(name = "messageSource")
        public ReloadableResourceBundleMessageSource messageSource() {
                ReloadableResourceBundleMessageSource messageBundle =
                                new ReloadableResourceBundleMessageSource();
                messageBundle.setBasename("classpath:messages/messages");
                messageBundle.setDefaultEncoding("UTF-8");
                return messageBundle;
        }
}
```

In Listing 2-22, you annotated the UserRegistrationConfiguration class with the @Configuration annotation. The bean name is defined as messageSource using @Bean(name = "messageSource").

The @Configuration annotation is a meta-annotation and indicates that this configuration class can have one or more @Bean methods to generate bean definitions manageable by the Spring container. This bean will allow you to alter a message's properties file without restarting the application.

The method messageSource configures a ReloadableResourceBundleMessageSource to support messages from properties. The ReloadableResourceBundleMessageSource bean is a kind of MessageSource that loads a message's properties file and resolves message keys from a properties file.

To set a base name, the setBaseName method takes an argument as classpath:messages/messages (in other words, the path of the property file). You set the default encoding of the message source file like UTF-8. Spring will search for a properties file named messages.properties in the src/main/resources/messages folder.

Create a Properties File

Let's create a messages.properties file under the src/main/resources/messages folder and add the following messages:

```
error.name.empty=The name is required field
error.name.length=The name should be limited to 50 characters
error.address.empty=The address is required field
error.address.length=The address should be limited to 150 characters
error.email.empty=The email is required field
error.email.email=The email should be in proper format
error.email.length=The email should be limited to 80 characters
```

These messages follow the specific pattern for each key of the message, as shown here:

```
error.<<field-name>>.<<constraint-name>>
```

Bean Validation Annotation with the message Attribute

Let's use the JSR-303 annotation for bean validation with the message attribute. The message attribute is used to set a custom error message to be displayed when the constraint defined by the annotation is not satisfied. Listing 2-23 shows the necessary code changes.

This message attribute will get the message value from the messages.properties file for the matched message key using the ReloadableResourceBundleMessageSource bean defined in the previous section.

Listing 2-23. Bean Validation Annotation with message Attribute

```
package com.apress.ravi.dto;

import javax.persistence.Column;
import javax.persistence.Entity;
import javax.persistence.GeneratedValue;
import javax.persistence.Id;

import org.hibernate.validator.constraints.Email;
import org.hibernate.validator.constraints.Length;
import org.hibernate.validator.constraints.NotEmpty;

@Entity
public class UsersDTO {

        @Id
        @GeneratedValue
        @Column(name = "USER_ID")
        private Long id;

        @NotEmpty(message = "error.name.empty")
        @Length(max = 50, message = "error.name.length")
        @Column(name = "NAME")
        private String name;

        @NotEmpty(message = "error.address.empty")
        @Length(max = 150, message = "error.address.length")
        @Column(name = "ADDRESS")
        private String address;

        @Email(message = "error.email.email")
        @NotEmpty(message = "error.email.empty")
        @Length(max = 80, message = "error.email.length")
        @Column(name = "EMAIL")
        private String email;

        //Getter & Setter method

}
```

Up to now you have created the ReloadableResourceBundleMessageSource bean and defined messages in the messages.properties file and annotated entity class with bean validation annotation with the message attribute.

The next step is to read messages from the properties file and use them during FieldValidationErrorinstance creation.

Reading Messages from the Properties File

To read the properties file, autowire the MessageSource by passing the argument in the constructor annotated with the @Autowired annotation of the RestValidationHandler class. Listing 2-24 shows the updated source code for the handleValidationError method in the RestValidationHandler class.

Listing 2-24. Reading Messages from Message's Properties File

```
package com.apress.ravi.Exception;

import java.awt.TrayIcon.MessageType;
import java.util.ArrayList;
import java.util.Date;
import java.util.List;

import javax.servlet.http.HttpServletRequest;

import org.springframework.beans.factory.annotation.Autowired;
import org.springframework.context.MessageSource;
import org.springframework.http.HttpStatus;
import org.springframework.http.ResponseEntity;
import org.springframework.validation.BindingResult;
import org.springframework.validation.FieldError;
import org.springframework.web.bind.MethodArgumentNotValidException;
import org.springframework.web.bind.annotation.ControllerAdvice;
import org.springframework.web.bind.annotation.ExceptionHandler;
import org.springframework.web.bind.annotation.ResponseStatus;

@ControllerAdvice
public class RestValidationHandler {

        private MessageSource messageSource;

        @Autowired
        public RestValidationHandler(MessageSource messageSource) {
                this.messageSource = messageSource;
        }

        // method to handle validation error
        @ExceptionHandler(MethodArgumentNotValidException.class)
        @ResponseStatus(HttpStatus.BAD_REQUEST)
        public ResponseEntity<FieldValidationErrorDetails> handleValidationError(
                        MethodArgumentNotValidException mNotValidException,
                        HttpServletRequest request) {
```

```
                FieldValidationErrorDetails fErrorDetails =
                                        new FieldValidationErrorDetails();

                fErrorDetails.setError_timeStamp(new Date().getTime());
                fErrorDetails.setError_status(HttpStatus.BAD_REQUEST.value());
                fErrorDetails.setError_title("Field Validation Error");
                fErrorDetails.setError_detail("Inut Field Validation Failed");
                fErrorDetails.setError_developer_Message(
                                mNotValidException.getClass().getName());
                fErrorDetails.setError_path(request.getRequestURI());

                BindingResult result = mNotValidException.getBindingResult();
                List<FieldError> fieldErrors = result.getFieldErrors();

                for (FieldError error : fieldErrors) {
                        FieldValidationError fError = processFieldError(error);
                        List<FieldValidationError> fValidationErrorsList =
                                fErrorDetails.getErrors().get(error.getField());
                        if (fValidationErrorsList == null) {
                                fValidationErrorsList =
                                        new ArrayList<FieldValidationError>();
                        }
                        fValidationErrorsList.add(fError);
                        fErrorDetails.getErrors().put(
                                error.getField(), fValidationErrorsList);
                }
                return new ResponseEntity<FieldValidationErrorDetails>(
                                fErrorDetails, HttpStatus.BAD_REQUEST);
        }

        // method to process field error
        private FieldValidationError processFieldError(final FieldError error) {
                FieldValidationError fieldValidationError =
                                        new FieldValidationError();
                if (error != null) {
                        Locale currentLocale = LocaleContextHolder.getLocale();
                        String msg = messageSource.getMessage(
                                error.getDefaultMessage(), null, currentLocale);
                        fieldValidationError.setFiled(error.getField());
                        fieldValidationError.setType(MessageType.ERROR);
                        fieldValidationError.setMessage(msg);
                }
                return fieldValidationError;
        }
}
```

In Listing 2-24, you used the getMessage method of MessageSource to retrieve messages from the properties file based on currentLocale.

To test the changes, restart the UserRegistrationSystem application and launch Postman to submit a user with a missing address and incorrect e-mail pattern, as shown in Figure 2-12. This will result in the new validation error message from the properties file.

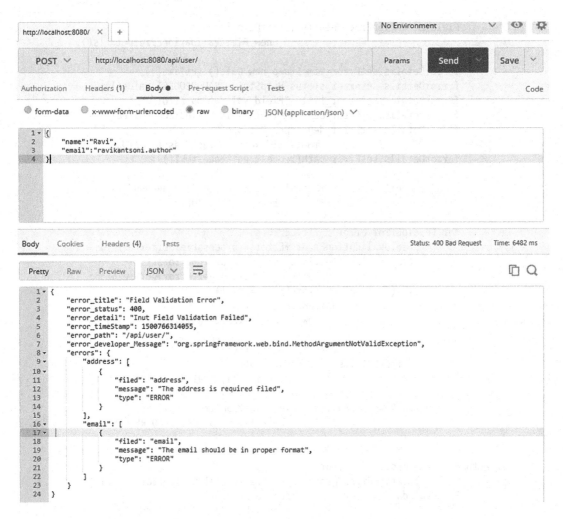

Figure 2-12. *Creating a user with a missing address and incorrect e-mail pattern*

Summary

In this chapter, you looked at creating RESTful services for the UserRegistrationSystem application. You now understand HTTP methods and status codes. You created different endpoints to perform CRUD operations. You handled errors in a RESTful API and defined a custom error response. You also validated request input using the Validation annotation and externalized error message.

In the next chapter, you will develop a single-page application using AngularJS to consume RESTful APIs.

■ ■ ■

CHAPTER 3

Setting Up AngularJS: Creating Your Single-Page Application

In the previous chapter, you looked at creating RESTful services for the UserRegistrationSystem application. You now understand HTTP methods and status codes. You created different endpoints to perform CRUD operations. You handled errors in the REST API and defined your custom error response. You also validated request input using the Validation annotation and externalized error messages.

The front end involves everything that the user sees, including the design and some languages like HTML and CSS. The main aim of the front-end code is to interact with the user, as well as present the data in a well-defined style. There are so many amazing JavaScript libraries that you can use when building a front-end application.

AngularJS is an open source JavaScript framework that provides structured methods for creating web applications. It is a JavaScript library built on the top of a light version of jQuery. It enforces a structured, clean Model-View-Controller (MVC) framework. AngularJS is a perfect solution for a client-side library for Spring Boot because of this clean and structured approach.

In this chapter, I will introduce MVC and the AngularJS framework and its major components so you can develop a front end for your UserRegistrationSystem application developed using Spring Boot.

I will start with an introduction of AngularJS and its life cycle. You will then look into AngularJS components and how to implement them in your application. Also, you will consume your REST API developed in Chapter 2 to develop your single-page application (SPA). In this chapter, you will learn about the following:

- How to use AngularJS as a front-end framework

- How to develop a single-page application to consume a REST API

In this chapter, you will learn how to integrate the AngularJS framework in your Spring Boot UserRegistrationSystem application to develop a single-page application. If you want to get an in-depth understanding of AngularJS, then refer to https://angularjs.org/.

Introducing AngularJS as a Front-End Framework

AngularJS is a library written in JavaScript for web application development, maintained by Google. It is an open source JavaScript framework and addresses the challenges of single-page applications (SPAs). An AngularJS web application follows the MVC design pattern, which results in developing extendable, maintainable, testable, and standardized web applications. AngularJS data binding and dependency injection make it an ideal partner with any server technology because it eliminates much of the code you would otherwise have to write, and it all happens within the browser.

© Ravi Kant Soni 2017
R. K. Soni, *Full Stack AngularJS for Java Developers*, https://doi.org/10.1007/978-1-4842-3198-2_3

AngularJS Basic Components

AngularJS allows developers to build structured applications based on the MVC model that are robust and easily maintained. It is important to get familiar with the various components of AngularJS before implementing AngularJS.

- *Module*: This is one of the components of AngularJS. A module is basically a container containing services, controllers, filters, directives, and so on. Each module in AngularJS has its own folder structure for controllers, directives, and so on. Each view page in AngularJS has a module.

- *Scope*: Scope in AngularJS is just a JavaScript representation of data used to populate a view on a web page. This data can be from any source such as a database or a remote web server.

- *View*: Views with templates and directives in AngularJS are other components of AngularJS to build an HTML view that is presented to the user.

- *Expression*: The ability to add an expression inside an HTML template is a great feature of AngularJS. An expression is basically linked to a scope. An expression helps bind application data to HTML.

- *Controller*: A controller is a component of the MVC framework. A controller will contain your core business logic. Its main role in AngularJS is to expose data to the view page using the scope.

- *Data binding*: An important feature of AngularJS is data binding. This is the process of linking data from the model to the view, and vice versa. AngularJS supports two-way data binding.

  - When data changes on a web page, the model is updated.

  - When data changes in the model, then the view page is automatically updated.

- The model represents the data, and the view projects the data.

- *Services*: Services in AngularJS are singleton objects that provide functionality for a web application.

- *Dependency injection*: DI is the process of injecting the dependency at runtime (i.e., making dependent components available for access within the component of initialized code). It is used to consume services. For example, if a module requires access to a resource via an HTTP request, then the HTTP service can be injected into the module to make the functionality available in the module code.

AngularJS Life Cycle

Now that you understand the different components involved in an AngularJS application, I'll cover what happens during the AngularJS life cycle, which has three phases: bootstrap, compilation, and runtime. These phases of AngularJS occur at the time of the web page being loaded in the client's browser. To design and implement the code in an application developed using AngularJS, it is important to understand the life cycle of AngularJS.

Bootstrap Phase

The bootstrap phase is the first phase of the AngularJS life cycle and occurs when the AngularJS JavaScript library is downloaded to the client's browser. Once the JavaScript library is downloaded, AngularJS initializes its own components and initializes the application's module, which the ng-app directive points to. The static DOM in this phase is loaded into the browser.

Compilation Phase

The HTML compilation stage is the second phase in the AngularJS life cycle. In this phase, the loaded static DOM is replaced with the dynamic DOM to represent the AngularJS view. Then these DOMs get linked to the appropriate JavaScript function from the AngularJS built-in library or custom directive code.

Runtime Data Binding Phase

This is the final stage of the AngularJS life cycle, which exists as long as the user does not reload or navigate away from a web page. In this phase, any changes made to the scope reflect in the view, and vice versa.

AngularJS Architecture Concepts

Now you will take a look at the architecture concept of AngularJS. When an HTML document is loaded into the browser and is evaluated by the browser, first the AngularJS JavaScript file is loaded, the Angular global object is created, and your JavaScript that registers the controller functions is executed. Then AngularJS scans the HTML looking for AngularJS apps and views and finds a controller function corresponding to the view. Then AngularJS executes the controller functions and updates the views with data from the model populated by the controller.

Next AngularJS listens for browser events, for example, a button clicked, a mouse moved, an input field being changed, and so on. If any of these events happen, then AngularJS will update the view accordingly. Figure 3-1 shows the workflow diagram of AngularJS.

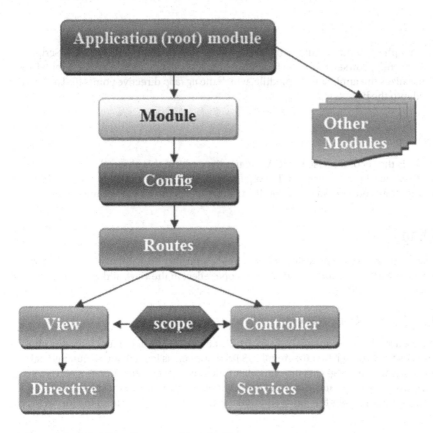

Figure 3-1. *Workflow diagram of AngularJS*

AngularJS contains a module that acts as a container for different types of applications such as views, controllers, directives, services, and so on. A module specifies how an application can be bootstrapped. Then you have a config component. The routes are used for linking URLs to controllers and views. A view is used to handle a sophisticated event. It uses ng-view directives. Also, you have a controller, which controls the data of the AngularJS application and consists of regular JavaScript objects. AngularJS defines an ng-controller directive that creates new controller objects by using a controller function. AngularJS comes with several built-in services such as $http, $route, $window, $location, and so on. The scope refers to the objects that refer to the model. They play the important role of joining the controller with the view.

MVC Architecture

AngularJS uses an MVC architecture to create web applications. The MVC architecture is a programming methodology that aims to split an application into three core components: a model, a view, and a controller. These three components combine to form your application. Figure 3-2 shows the Model-View-Controller architecture.

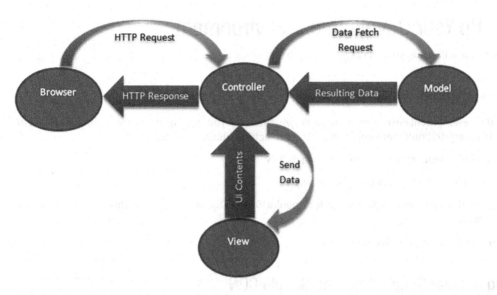

Figure 3-2. *MVC architecture in AngularJS*

When a user sends an HTTP request via a browser, the request is received by the controller. The controller processes that request and sends the request to the model to provide the appropriate data. The model in response provides the resulting data array to the controller again. The controller processes the data again to the required format and sends it to the view. The view represents the data via UI contents and sends it to the controller. Finally, the controller sends the HTTP response to the browser.

- *AngularJS views* are used to generate an output representation of information, such as a chart or a diagram, to the user in a web browser. AngularJS builds the views in the DOM by pulling in all the templates defined for an application. So, the developer work here is to just create the template by using mostly HTML and CSS.

- The *AngularJS model* contains the $scope object that is used to store the application model, so there's no need to create a JavaScript model class like with other JavaScript client-side frameworks. Scopes are attached to the DOM, helping to simplify the JavaScript problem considerably.

- The *AngularJS controller* is the place where you define all the business logic specific to a particular view. The controller holds the model and view together.

Setting Up Your Development Environment

In this section, you will set up your development environment.

Adding AngularJS to Spring Boot

Let's set up the development environment by adding AngularJS to your Spring Boot application developed in Chapter 2's UserRegistrationSystem application. You can achieve this in three ways.

- Include Angular scripts from the Google CDN

- Download and host Angular files locally

- Provide dependency information for AngularJS in the Spring Boot application's `pom.xml`

The following sections will cover all three ways.

Including Angular Scripts from the Google CDN

Here's how you include your Angular scripts from the Google CDN.

To get started quickly with AngularJS, point your HTML `<script>` tag to a Google CDN URL. Two types of Angular script URLs are available, one for production and one for development.

- `angular.min.js`: This is minified version that should be used in production.

- `angular.js`: This is nonminified, human-readable version that should be used in web development.

Listing 3-1 shows an example of pointing your code to the minified version 1.5.6 of an Angular script on the Google CDN server.

Listing 3-1. H2 pom.xml Dependency

```
<!doctype html>
<html ng-app>
  <head>
    <title>Angular Application</title>
    <script src="https://ajax.googleapis.com/ajax/libs/angularjs/1.5.6/angular.min.js"></
script>
  </head>
  <body>
  </body>
</html>
```

Downloading and Hosting Angular Files Locally

Another way to include Angular scripts is by downloading and hosting Angular files locally.

A developer who wants to work with Angular offline or wants to host Angular files on their own server can opt for this option. Navigate to `https://code.angularjs.org/` and download the required version from the list of Angular versions. Or you can download the latest stable release of Angular from `https://angularjs.org/`. Figure 3-3 shows the AngularJS page with the download link.

Figure 3-3. *AngularJS page*

Click Download AngularJS to display a pop-up to download AngularJS, as shown in Figure 3-4.

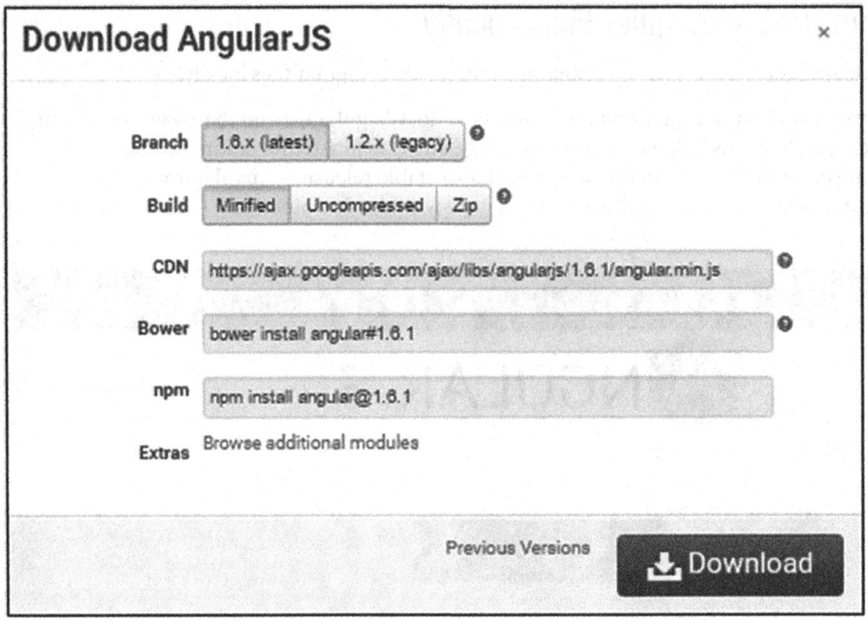

Figure 3-4. *Pop-up to download AngularJS*

Providing Dependency Information in pom.xml

Instead of manually downloading the AngularJS library, you can provide dependency information for AngularJS in pom.xml while developing a Spring Boot application so that AngularJS will be automatically downloaded to the library. Listing 3-2 shows the dependency information for AngularJS and Bootstrap for CSS.

Listing 3-2. Added Dependency for AngularJS and Bootstrap in pom.xml

```
<dependency>
        <groupId>org.webjars</groupId>
        <artifactId>angularjs</artifactId>
        <version>1.4.9</version>
        <scope>runtime</scope>
</dependency>
<dependency>
        <groupId>org.webjars</groupId>
        <artifactId>bootstrap</artifactId>
        <version>3.3.6</version>
        <scope>runtime</scope>
</dependency>
```

Adding Twitter Bootstrap to Spring Boot

Twitter Bootstrap is a front-end framework that was created to make responsive design much easier. The Bootstrap CSS framework can be used to style the content of a web site. You can create your own CSS styles to make your web site look awesome, but Bootstrap provides a nice set of CSS styles that will let you design a really great-looking content layout. It is not really required to use Bootstrap while working with AngularJS, and there is no intrinsic relationship between AngularJS and Bootstrap as both are different packages.

To use CSS from the Bootstrap CSS framework, you can define a dependency in pom.xml while developing a Spring Boot application, as shown in Listing 3-2, so that it will be automatically downloaded to the library folder. Also, the Bootstrap archive can be downloaded from https://getbootstrap.com/, which also contains CSS and JavaScript files.

Developing Your Single-Page Application

Single-page applications are applications that have one entry point HTML page (may be index.html); all the application content is dynamically added to and removed from that one page. At runtime, based on some event, existing content attached to the tag is removed, and dynamic content is then attached to the same tag.

The entry point of a single-page application can be seen in an index.html that contains a <div ng-view></div> tag, as shown in Listing 3-3, where all the dynamic content is inserted into index. html. So, rather than a user waiting for a new page to load, new content is dynamically displayed in a fraction of the time.

Listing 3-3. Developing the HTML Page: Entry Point of a Single-Page Application

```
<!DOCTYPE html>
<html lang="en" ng-app="userregistrationsystem">
<head>
        ...
</head>
<body>
        ...
        <div ng-view></div>
        ...
        <script src="/webjars/angularjs/1.4.9/angular.js"></script>
        <script src="/webjars/angularjs/1.4.9/angular-resource.js"></script>
        <script src="/webjars/angularjs/1.4.9/angular-route.js"></script>
        <script src="/js/app.js"></script>
        <script src="/js/controller.js"></script>
        <link rel="stylesheet"
                href="/webjars/bootstrap/3.3.6/css/bootstrap.css">
</body>
</html>
```

In Listing 3-3, you are using these good practices while developing the HTML page:

- Place the <script> tag at the bottom of the page to improve the app load time because the loading of the Angular script will not affect the HTML loading.

- Place ng-app at the root of your application, typically on the <html> tag if you want Angular to autobootstrap your application.

Bootstrapping the Application

Bootstrapping AngularJS is the process of initialization, or starting, your Angular app by adding ng-app to an element in your HTML, as shown in Listing 3-4, when an application first starts.

Listing 3-4. Bootstrapping AngularJS by Adding ng-app in an HTML Page

```
<html lang="en" ng-app="userregistrationsystem">
...
</html>
```

This is also known as *automatic initialization*. So, when AngularJS finds the ng-app directive after analyzing the index.html file, it loads the associated modules and then compiles the DOM.

The AngularJS application UserRegistrationSystem is defined as the AngularJS module (angular.module) in app.js, which is the entry point into the application.

```
var app = angular.module('userregistrationsystem', ['ngRoute', 'ngResource']);
```

The variable app in the app.js file could be named anything.

Dependency Injection

Dependency injection is a design pattern to define dependencies in an application as part of configuration instead of hard-coding them within the component. DI helps you avoid the manual creation of application dependencies and makes it possible to change them whenever needed. AngularJS uses DI to load module dependencies when an application first starts.

The benefits of DI are as follows:

- It separates the process of creating dependencies and their consumption.

- The consumer will feel like the process of creating dependencies is being handled by someone else; the user just needs to worry about how to use the dependency.

- It offers the facility to change the dependencies whenever needed.

- It makes an application more testable.

As you can see, the two dependencies have been defined in app.js as needed by userregistrationsystem at startup, as shown here:

```
var app = angular.module('userregistrationsystem', ['ngRoute', 'ngResource']);
```

The two dependencies in the previous code are defined in an array in the module definition.

- ngRoute: The first dependency is the AngularJS ngRoute module, which provides routing to the application. The ngRoute module is used for deep-linking URLs to controllers and views (HTML partials).

- ngResource: The second dependency is the AngularJS ngResource module, which provides interaction support with RESTful services.

AngularJS Routes

AngularJS routes are configured using the $routeProvider API. Routes are dependent on the ngRoute module, which is why its dependency is defined in an array in the module definition.

Listing 3-5 shows the code from app.js. You will define four routes in your AngularJS application.

- The first is /list-all-users.

- The second one is /register-new-user.

- The third one is /update-user/:id.

- The fourth one is different from the other three.

Listing 3-5. Defining Routes in AngularJS Application

```
app.config(function($routeProvider) {
        $routeProvider
                .when('/list-all-users', {
                        templateUrl : '/template/listuser.html',
                        controller : 'listUserController'
                }).when('/register-new-user',{
                        templateUrl : '/template/userregistration.html',
                        controller : 'registerUserController'
                }).when('/update-user/:id',{
                        templateUrl : '/template/userupdation.html' ,
                        controller : 'usersDetailsController'
                }).otherwise({
                        redirectTo : '/home',
                        templateUrl : '/template/home.html',
                });
});
```

The four defined routes in Listing 3-5 map directly to URLs defined in the application.

When the user clicks the link in the application specified at http://localhost:8080/#/list-all-users, the /list-all-users route will be followed, and the content associated with the /list-all-users URL will be displayed.

Similarly, when the user clicks the link http://localhost:8080/#/register-new-user, the /register-new-user route will be followed, and the content associated with /register-new-user URL will be displayed.

When the user clicks the link http://localhost:8080/#/update-user/{id}, the /update-user/:id route will be followed, and the content associated with the /update-user/:id URL will be displayed.

Also, if the user accesses any URL other than these three, the /home route will be followed, and the content associated with the /home URL will be displayed.

AngularJS Templates

AngularJS templates, also known as *HTML partials*, are HTML code that are bound to the <div ng-view> </div> tag shown in the index.html file. If you look at the code from the app.js file, you can see that different templateUrl values are defined for different routes, as shown in Listing 3-6.

71

Listing 3-6. Defining templateUrl for Routes

```
$routeProvider
        .when('/list-all-users', {
                templateUrl : '/template/listuser.html',
                controller : 'listUserController'
        }).when('/register-new-user',{
                templateUrl : '/template/userregistration.html',
                controller : 'registerUserController'
        }).when('/update-user/:id',{
                templateUrl : '/template/userupdation.html' ,
                controller : 'usersDetailsController'
        }).otherwise({
                redirectTo : '/home',
                templateUrl : '/template/home.html',
        });
```

As shown in Listing 3-6, you have defined four different partials or templates. The listuser.html, userregistration.html, userupdation.html, and home.html pages are four different partials or templates, which contain HTML code and AngularJS's built-in template language to display dynamic data in your template.

Implementing the Model, View, and Controller in Your Single-Page Application

Spring Boot, by default, will automatically serve static content from the root of ServletContext or from the following directories:

- classpath:/META-INF/resources/

- classpath:/resources/

- classpath:/static/

- classpath:/public/

In your project, you will be creating the static content under the classpath:/resources/ directory. The final directory structure will look like Figure 3-5.

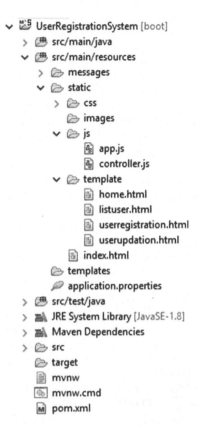

Figure 3-5. *Directory structure of SPA in the UserRegistrationSystem application*

Let's implement the model, view, and controller in your AngularJS application.

Create the Home/Application Page

The core of a single-page application is the static page index.html, as shown in Listing 3-7, so let's create it in the src/main/resources/static (or src/main/resources/public) directory. This index.html page will contain some front-end code to display links on the web page, which will be handled by AngularJS. This src/main/resources/static/index.html page also contains some <script> tags that include all the necessary AngularJS files.

Listing 3-7. src/main/resources/static/index.html

```
<!DOCTYPE html>
<html lang="en" ng-app="userregistrationsystem">
<head>
<title>Full Stack Development</title>
<link rel="stylesheet" href="/css/app.css">
</head>
```

```
<body>
        <div class="page-header text-center">
                <h2>User Registration System</h2>
        </div>
        <nav class="navbar navbar-default">
                <div class="container-fluid">
                        <a href="#/"
                                class="btn btn-info navbar-btn"
                                role="button">
                                        Home
                        </a>
                        <a href="#/register-new-user"
                                class="btn btn-info navbar-btn"
                                role="button">
                                        Register New User
                        </a>
                        <a href="#/list-all-users"
                                class="btn btn-info"
                                role="button">
                                        List All Users
                        </a>
                </div>
        </nav>
        <div ng-view></div>
        <script src="/webjars/angularjs/1.4.9/angular.js"></script>
        <script src="/webjars/angularjs/1.4.9/angular-resource.js"></script>
        <script src="/webjars/angularjs/1.4.9/angular-route.js"></script>
        <script src="/js/app.js"></script>
        <script src="/js/controller.js"></script>
        <link rel="stylesheet"
                href="/webjars/bootstrap/3.3.6/css/bootstrap.css">
</body>
</html>
```

This index.html page will display three links: Home, Register New User, and List All Users.

Let's look at the previous code in more detail. The AngularJS library enables several custom attributes for use with standard HTML tags.

- The <html> tag in the index.html page has the ng-app="userregistrationsystem" that tells you to define a JavaScript module that Angular will recognize as an application called userregistrationsystem.

- All the CSS classes are from (Twitter) Bootstrap to make the page look pretty.

- Angular JS and (Twitter) Bootstrap are included at the bottom of the <body> tag, as shown in the previous code, so that the browser can process the entire HTML before it gets processed.

- You have also included a separate app.js, which is where you will be defining the application behavior.

Create the View Pages

Let's create four view pages in the template folder inside the src/main/resources/static directory.

- *Home page*: src/main/resources/template/home.html

- *Register New User page*: src/main/resources/template/userregistration.html

- *List Of User page*: src/main/resources/template/listuser.html

- *Update Existing User page*: src/main/resources/template/userupdation.html

Home Page

Listing 3-8 shows the code for the home.html view page. This page is created inside the folder src/main/resources/template.

Listing 3-8. src/main/resources/template/home.html

```
<div class="container">
        <div class="panel panel-default ">
                <div class="alert alert-success">
                        <span class="lead">
                                Welcome to User Registration System
                        </span>
                </div>
                <div class="panel-body ">
                        <div class="alert alert-info">
                                <ul>
                                        <li>
                                                Please click on
                                                <strong>Register New User</strong>
                                                to register a new user.
                                        </li>
                                        <li>
                                                Please click on
                                                <strong>List All Users</strong>
                                                to get all users.
                                        </li>
                                </ul>
                        </div>
                </div>
        </div>
</div >
```

In the home.html page, you are just displaying a (static) welcome message to user, as shown in Figure 3-6.

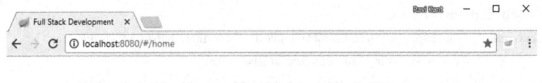

Figure 3-6. *Home page*

Register New User Page

Listing 3-9 shows the code for the userregistration.html view page. This page is created inside the folder src/main/resources/template.

Listing 3-9. src/main/resources/template/userregistration.html

```
<div class="container">
 <div class="alert alert-danger" role="alert" ng-if="errorMessage">
  {{errorMessage}}
 </div>
 <div class="panel panel-default ">
  <div class="alert alert-success">
   <span class="lead">Register New User</span>
    <p>Please maintain uniqueness of User-Name</p>
   </div>
  <div class="panel-body ">
   <div class="container">
        <form ng-submit="submitUserForm()" name="myForm"
         class="form-horizontal">
          <div class="row">
               <div class="form-group col-md-12">
                <label class="col-md-2 control-lable" for="uname">
                  Name
                </label>
```

```
                <div class="col-md-7">
                        <input type="text" ng-model="user.name"
                                id="uname" class="form-control input-sm"
                                placeholder="Enter user name" />
                </div>
                </div>
        </div>
        <div class="row">
                <div class="form-group col-md-12">
                  <label class="col-md-2 control-lable" for="address">
                        Address
                  </label>
                  <div class="col-md-7">
                        <input type="text" ng-model="user.address"
                                id="address" class="form-control input-sm"
                                placeholder="Enter User Address." />
                  </div>
                </div>
        </div>
        <div class="row">
                <div class="form-group col-md-12">
                  <label class="col-md-2 control-lable" for="email">
                        Email
                  </label>
                  <div class="col-md-7">
                        <input type="email" ng-model="user.email"
                                id="email" class="form-control input-sm"
                                placeholder="Enter User Email" />
                  </div>
                </div>
        </div>
        <div class="row">
                <div class="form-actions floatRight">
                        <input type="submit" value="Register User"
                                class="btn btn-primary btn-sm">
                        <button type="button" ng-click="resetForm()"
                                class="btn btn-warning btn-sm">Reset Form</button>
                </div>
        </div>
      </form>
   </div>
  </div>
 </div>
</div>
```

In the userregistration.html page (as shown in the previous code), errorMessage is marked up using curly braces, as in {{errorMessage}}. These curly braces will be filled in later by AngularJS using a controller defined in the app.js file.

You have also created input boxes to enter the name, address, and e-mail. Once a user enters the details and clicks the Register User button, the user details will be saved in the database.

You have a Reset Form button that will reset the input box with an empty value. Figure 3-7 shows the view of the Register New User page in the browser.

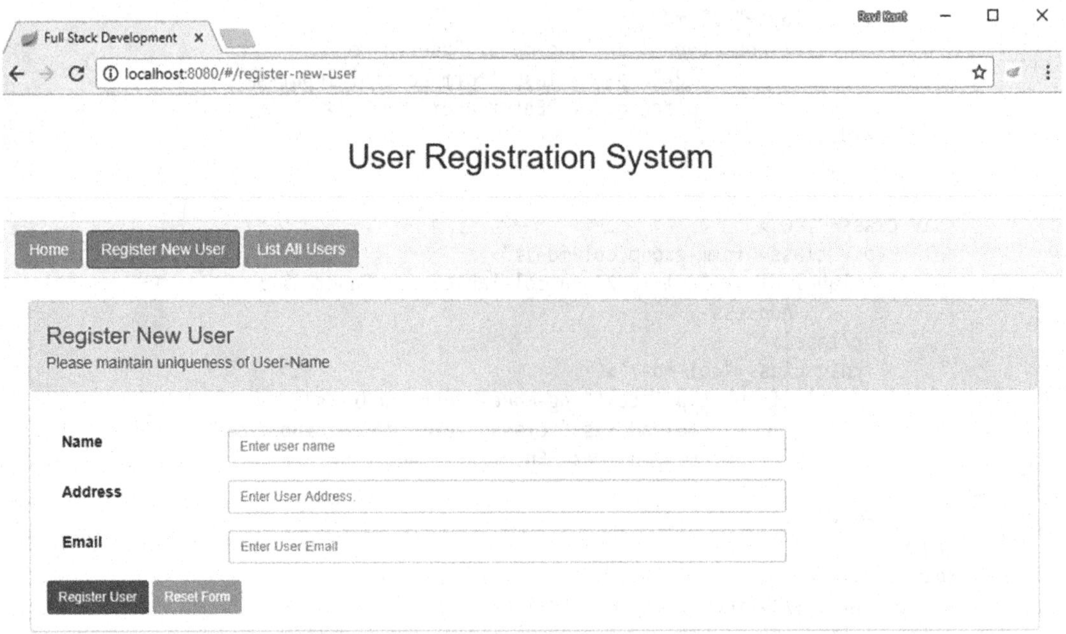

Figure 3-7. *Register New User page*

Once the user successfully performs the user registration by entering the correct details and a unique name, as shown in Figure 3-8, then the user will be navigated to the List All Users page.

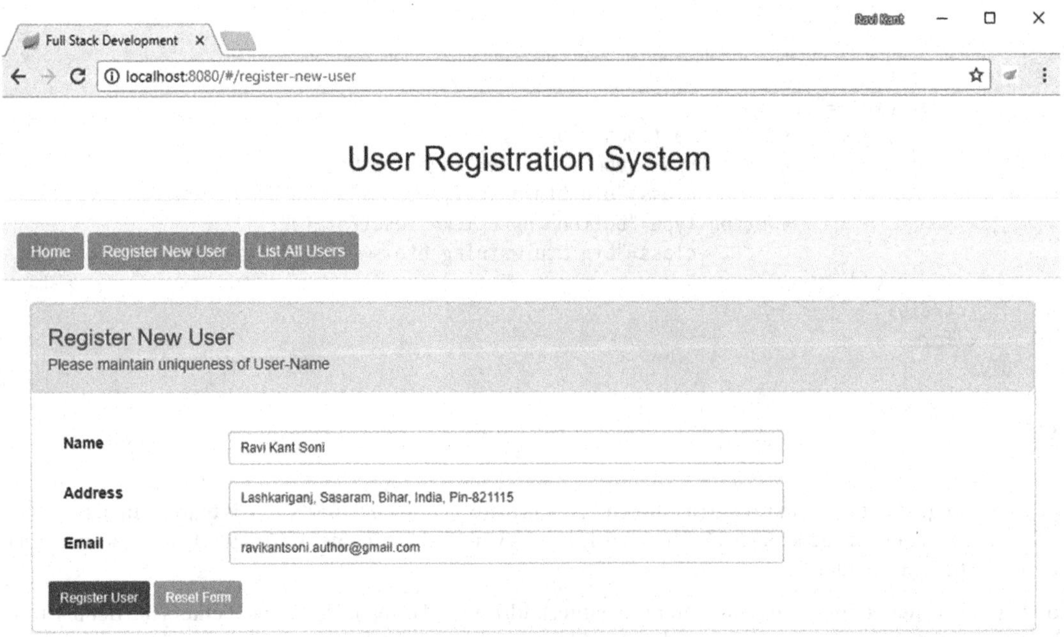

Figure 3-8. *Registering a new user with the user's details*

If the username entered is not unique and if the user with the matching name exists in the database, then a warning error message will be displayed in the browser, as shown in Figure 3-9.

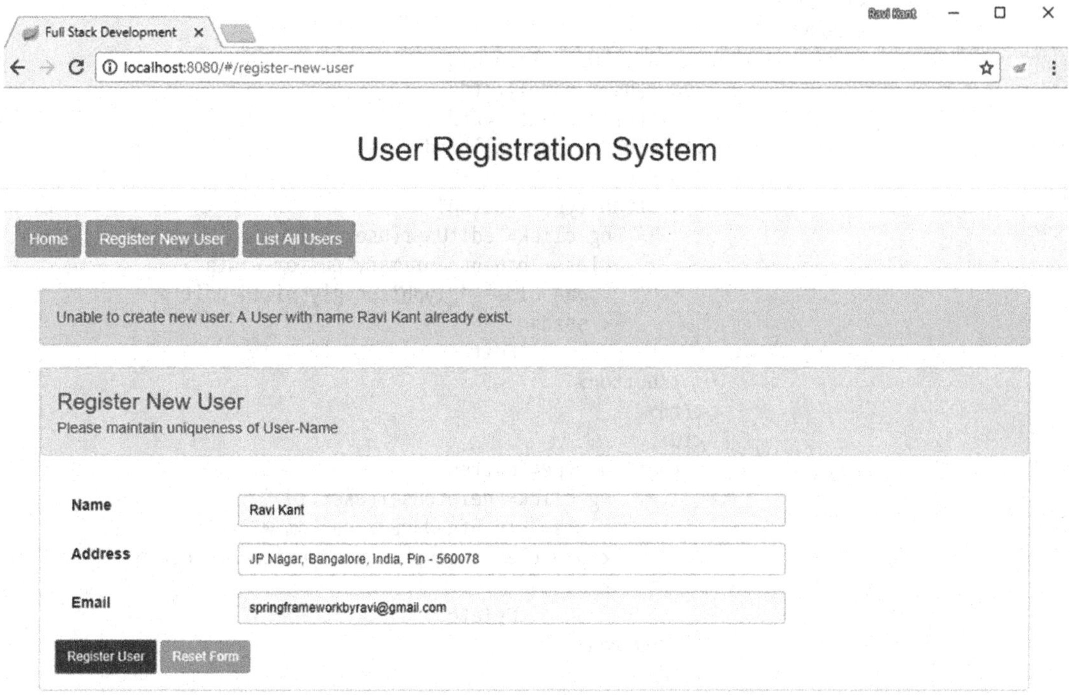

Figure 3-9. *Error message on duplicate username*

List of Users

Listing 3-10 shows the code for the listuser.html view page. This page is created inside the folder src/main/resources/template. This page will show the list of all users in the UserRegistrationSystem application.

Listing 3-10. src/main/resources/template/listuser.html

```
<div class="container">
  <div class="panel panel-default ">
      <div class="alert alert-info">
        <span class="lead">List of Users </span>
      </div>
      <div class="panel-body ">
        <div class="table-responsive">
              <table class="table table-hover table-bordered ">
              <thead>
                    <tr>
                      <th>Name</th>
                      <th>Email</th>
                      <th>Address</th>
```

```html
                        <th width="100">Edit</th>
                        <th width="100">Delete</th>
                    </tr>
                </thead>
                <tbody>
                    <tr ng-repeat="user in users">
                        <td>{{user.name}}</td>
                        <td>{{user.email}}</td>
                        <td>{{user.address}}</td>
                        <td>
                          <button type="button"
                                  ng-click="editUser(user.id)"
                                  class="btn btn-primary custom-width">
                                  <span class="glyphicon glyphicon-edit">
                                  </span>
                                          Edit
                          </button>
                        </td>
                        <td>
                          <button type="button"
                                  ng-click="deleteUser(user.id)"
                                  class="btn btn-danger custom-width">
                                  <span class="glyphicon glyphicon-remove">
                                  </span>
                                          Delete
                          </button>
                        </td>
                    </tr>
                </tbody>
            </table>
          </div>
        </div>
    </div>
</div>
```

In the listuser.html page (as shown in the previous code), the user.name, user.email, and user.address are marked up using curly braces: {{user.name}}, {{user.email}}, and {{user.address}}. These curly braces will be filled in later by AngularJS using a controller defined in the app.js file.

This page shows the list of all users in a table with the columns Name, Email, and Address and also contains Edit and Delete buttons. Figure 3-10 shows the view of the listuser.html page in the browser.

Figure 3-10. *List of users*

Clicking the Delete button will delete the specific user from the user table. Clicking the Edit button will redirect to the Update Existing User page.

Update Existing User

Listing 3-11 shows the code for the userupdation.html view page. This page is created inside the folder src/main/resources/template. This page allows you to update the existing user from the UserRegistrationSystem application.

Listing 3-11. src/main/resources/template/userupdation.html

```
<div class="container">
  <div class="alert alert-danger" role="alert" ng-if="errorMessage">
      {{errorMessage}}
  </div>
  <div class="panel panel-default ">
      <div class="alert alert-success">
        <span class="lead">Update Existing User</span>
        <p>Please maintain uniqueness of User-Name</p>
      </div>
      <div class="panel-body ">
        <div class="container">
              <form ng-submit="submitUserForm()" name="myForm"
                          class="form-horizontal">
                    <div class="row">
                          <div class="form-group col-md-12">
                                <label class="col-md-2 control-lable"
                                      for="uname">
                                          Name
                                </label>
```

81

```
                                        <div class="col-md-7">
                                          <input type="text" ng-model="user.name"
                                            id="uname" class="form-control input-sm"
                                            placeholder="Enter user name" />
                                        </div>
                                    </div>
                                </div>
                                <div class="row">
                                        <div class="form-group col-md-12">
                                                <label class="col-md-2 control-lable"
                                                        for="address">Address</label>
                                                <div class="col-md-7">
                                                 <input type="text" ng-model="user.address"
                                                    id="address" class="form-control input-sm"
                                                    placeholder="Enter User Address." />
                                                </div>
                                        </div>
                                </div>
                                <div class="row">
                                        <div class="form-group col-md-12">
                                                <label class="col-md-2 control-lable"
                                                        for="email">Email</label>
                                                <div class="col-md-7">
                                                  <input type="email" ng-model="user.email"
                                                    id="email" class="form-control input-sm"
                                                    placeholder="Enter User Email" />
                                                </div>
                                        </div>
                                </div>
                                <div class="row">
                                        <div class="form-actions floatRight">
                                          <input type="submit" value="Update User"
                                            class="btn btn-primary btn-sm">
                                          <button type="button" ng-click="resetForm()"
                                            class="btn btn-warning btn-sm"> Reset Form
                                            </button>
                                        </div>
                                </div>
                        </form>
                    </div>
                </div>
            </div>
        </div>
```

Figure 3-11 shows the view of the userupdation.html page in the browser when clicking the Edit button in the List Of Users table in Figure 3-10.

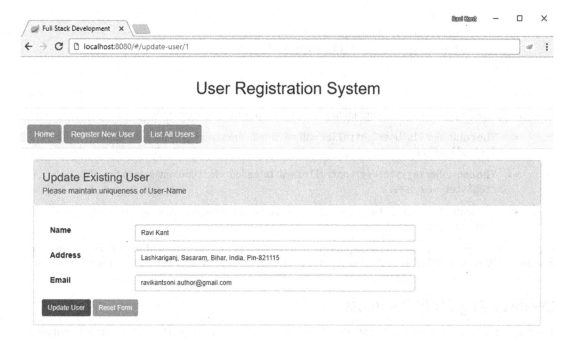

Figure 3-11. *Updating the user*

Once you update the user details along with the username and click the Update User button, you will navigate to the List of Users view.

Up to here, you are good with view pages. Now, you will be creating the UserRegistrationSystem application in the app.js file inside the js folder for your single-page application.

Create an AngularJS Application

Let's create an AngularJS application named as app in the src/main/resources/static/js/app.js file that defines the application module configuration and routes. To handle a request like /home, it needs an AngularJS module, called ngRoute. To use ngRoute and inject it into your application, you use angular. module to add the ngRoute module to your app, as shown in Listing 3-12.

Listing 3-12. src/main/resources/static/js/app.js

```
var app = angular.module('userregistrationsystem', ['ngRoute', 'ngResource']);

app.config(function($routeProvider) {
        $routeProvider.when('/list-all-users', {
                templateUrl : '/template/listuser.html',
                controller : 'listUserController'
        }).when('/register-new-user',{
                templateUrl : '/template/userregistration.html',
                controller : 'registerUserController'
        }).when('/update-user/:id',{
                templateUrl : '/template/userupdation.html' ,
                controller : 'usersDetailsController'
```

```
        }).otherwise({
                redirectTo : '/home',
                templateUrl : '/template/home.html',
        });
});
```

Then, in app.config, each route is mapped to a template and controller (optional).

- The controller listUserController will be called when you navigate to the URL /
  list-all-users.

- The controller registerUserController will be called when you navigate to the URL
  /register-new-user.

- The controller usersDetailsController will be called when you navigate to the URL
  /update-user/:id.

In this section, you have created the app application in the app.js file. Let's create three different controllers named listUserController, registerUserController, and usersDetailsController in the next section.

Create an AngularJS Controller

The controller.js file defined in the src/main/resources/static/js folder contains the implementation of AngularJS controllers.

Let's create an AngularJS controller module named registerUserController that will consume the Spring REST service to perform the POST HTTP call. Here, an errorMessage is set in $scope to display as an error message returned from the POST call to the server on the Register New User page. On a successful POST call, it will redirect to list-all-users. See Listing 3-13.

Listing 3-13. registerUserController in src/main/resources/static/js.controller.js

```
app.controller('registerUserController', function($scope, $http, $location,
            $route) {

      $scope.submitUserForm = function() {
            $http({
                    method : 'POST',
                    url : 'http://localhost:8080/api/user/',
                    data : $scope.user,
            }).then(function(response) {
                    $location.path("/list-all-users");
                    $route.reload();
            }, function(errResponse) {
                    $scope.errorMessage = errResponse.data.errorMessage;
            });
      }

      $scope.resetForm = function() {
            $scope.user = null;
      };
});
```

Similarly, you have defined listUserController and usersDetailsController to consume the REST API developed in Chapter 2. Listing 3-14 shows listUserController, and Listing 3-15 shows usersDetailsController.

Listing 3-14. listUserController in src/main/resources/static/js.controller.js

```
app.controller('listUserController', function($scope, $http, $location, $route) {
            $http({
                    method : 'GET',
                    url : 'http://localhost:8080/api/user/'
            }).then(function(response) {
                    $scope.users = response.data;
            });

            $scope.editUser = function(userId) {
                    $location.path("/update-user/" + userId);
            }

            $scope.deleteUser = function(userId) {
                    $http({
                            method : 'DELETE',
                            url : 'http://localhost:8080/api/user/' + userId
                    })
                                    .then(
                                                function(response) {
                                                        $location.path("/list-all-
                                                        users");
                                                        $route.reload();
                                    });

            }
});
```

Listing 3-15. usersDetailsController in src/main/resources/static/js.controller.js

```
app.controller('usersDetailsController',function($scope, $http, $location, $routeParams,
$route) {

        $scope.userId = $routeParams.id;

        $http({
                method : 'GET',
                url : 'http://localhost:8080/api/user/' + $scope.userId
        }).then(function(response) {
                $scope.user = response.data;
        });

        $scope.submitUserForm = function() {
                $http({
                        method : 'POST',
                        url : 'http://localhost:8080/api/user/',
                        data : $scope.user,
                })
```

```
                              .then(
                                    function(response) {
                                          $location.path("/list-all-users");
                                          $route.reload();
                                    },
                                    function(errResponse) {
                                          $scope.errorMessage = "Error while
                                          updating User - Error Message: '"
                                                      + errResponse.data.
                                                      errorMessage;
                              });
            }
});
```

Let's understand the code defined in the controller.js file. The controller module in controller.js is simply a function that takes different parameters based on the application requirements.

- $scope: $scope is used to set up dynamic content for the UI elements that this controller is responsible for. The concept of $scope is important in AngularJS as it can be seen as the glue that allows the template, model, and controller to work together. AngularJS supports dependency injection by naming conventions. AngularJS uses this $scope to keep the model and view separate but in sync. Any changes made in the view are reflected in the model, and any changes made in the model are reflected in the view.

- $http: The $http service is the core feature provided by AngularJS and is used to consume the REST service.

Running a Spring Boot Application in STS

Figure 3-12 shows the final directory structure of your UserRegistrationSystem application.

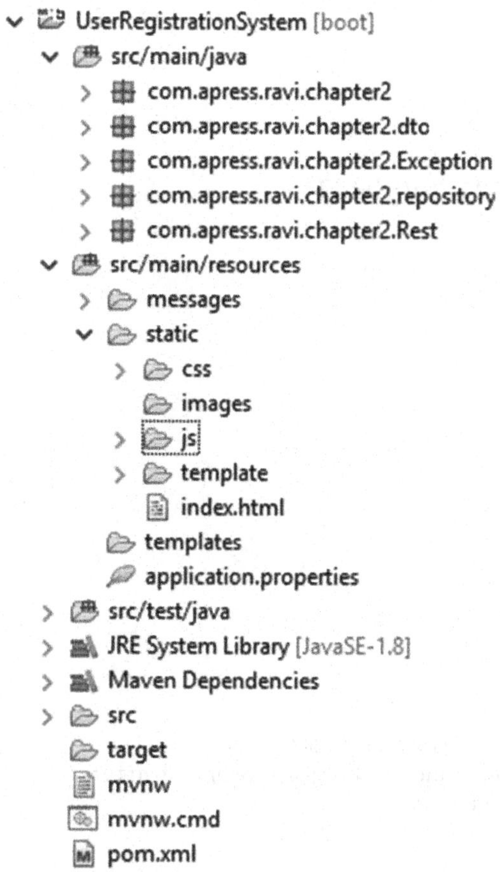

- ∨ 🗁 UserRegistrationSystem [boot]
  - ∨ 🗁 src/main/java
    - › ⊞ com.apress.ravi.chapter2
    - › ⊞ com.apress.ravi.chapter2.dto
    - › ⊞ com.apress.ravi.chapter2.Exception
    - › ⊞ com.apress.ravi.chapter2.repository
    - › ⊞ com.apress.ravi.chapter2.Rest
  - ∨ 🗁 src/main/resources
    - › 🗁 messages
    - ∨ 🗁 static
      - › 🗁 css
        - 🗁 images
      - › 🗁 js
      - › 🗁 template
        - 📄 index.html
    - 🗁 templates
    - 🔗 application.properties
  - › 🗁 src/test/java
  - › ▣ JRE System Library [JavaSE-1.8]
  - › ▣ Maven Dependencies
  - › 🗁 src
    - 🗁 target
    - 📄 mvnw
    - 📄 mvnw.cmd
    - 📄 pom.xml

Figure 3-12. *Directory structure of the UserRegistrationSystem application*

Let's run your UserRegistrationSystem application in STS. Congratulations! You have successfully set up and run the single-page application using Spring Boot and AngularJS. Now it's time to visit the URL in the browser to see the web page shown in Figure 3-13.

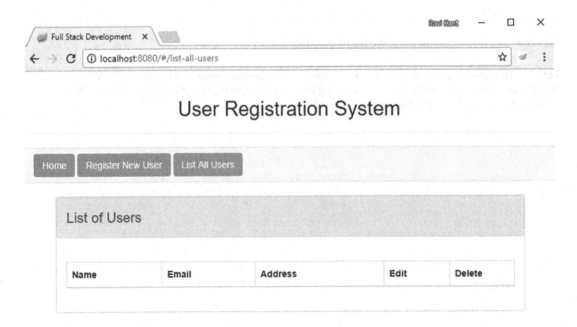

Figure 3-13. `http://localhost:8080/#/home`

By default, the web page will redirect to the home page (`http://localhost:8080/#/home`) that you have configured in `app.js`. Clicking the List All Users button on the home page will redirect to `http://localhost:8080/#/list-all-users`, as shown in Figure 3-14.

Figure 3-14. `http://localhost:8080/#/list-all-users`

This list is empty as of now; no user has been registered to the UserRegistrationSystem application. Let's register a new user by clicking the button Register New User. By clicking this button, it will redirect you to http://localhost:8080/#/register-new-user, as shown in Figure 3-15.

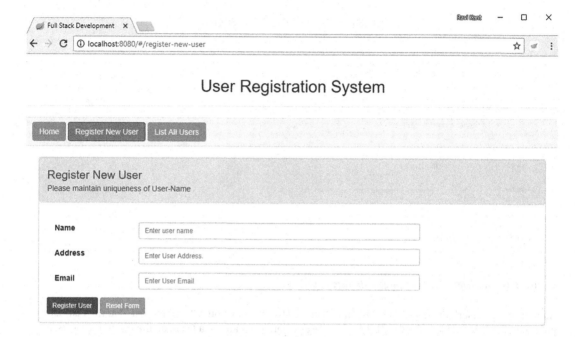

Figure 3-15. http://localhost:8080/#/register-new-user

The Register New User page contains an input box where you need to enter the name, address, and e-mail, as shown in Figure 3-16.

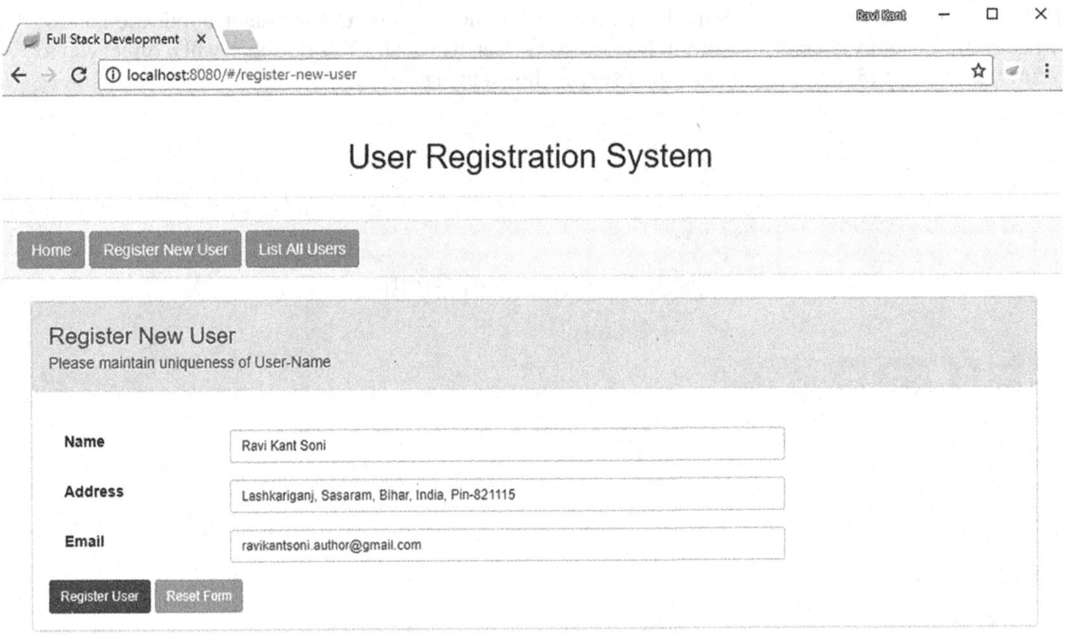

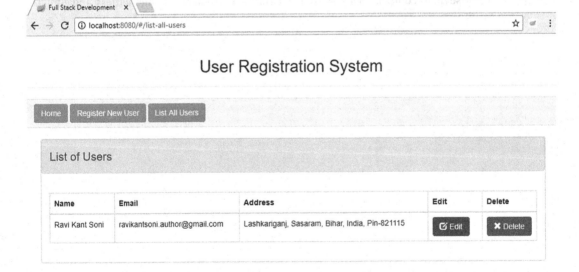

Figure 3-16. *Register New User page with user details*

After entering a user's details and clicking the Register User button, you will be redirected to the List User page at `http://localhost:8080/#/list-all-users` where you can see a list of all the registered users, as shown in Figure 3-17.

Figure 3-17. `http://localhost:8080/#/list-all-users`

The user table on the List of Users page contains the columns Name, Email, and Address and Edit and Delete buttons. Clicking Edit will allow you to edit a specific user's details, as shown in Figure 3-18.

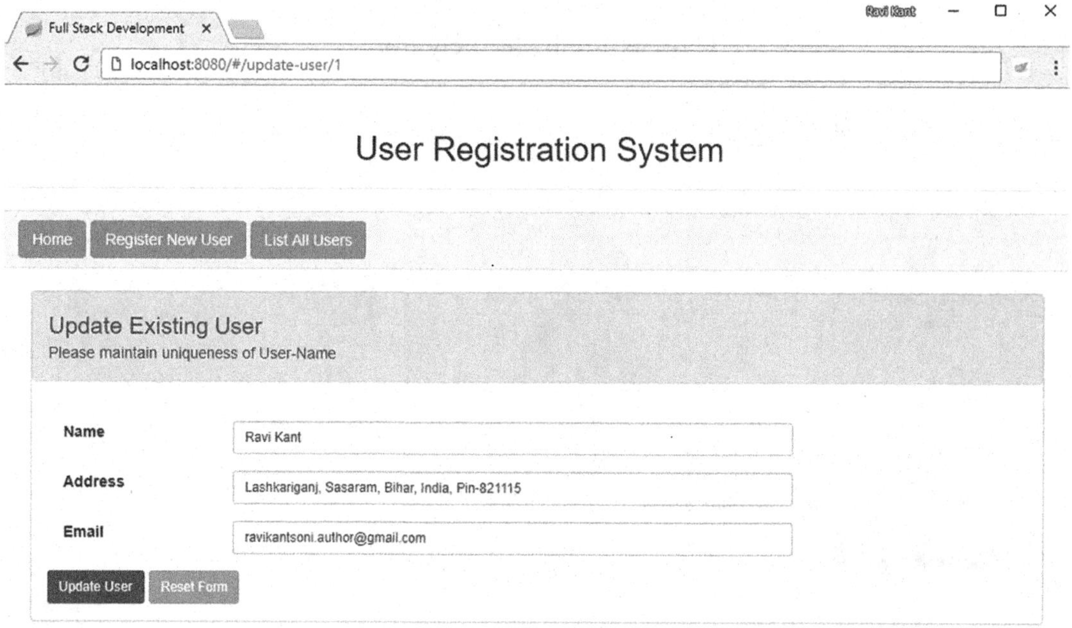

Figure 3-18. *http://localhost:8080/#/update-user/1*

If you try to register a new user with an existing username, then an error message will be displayed on the page, as shown in Figure 3-19.

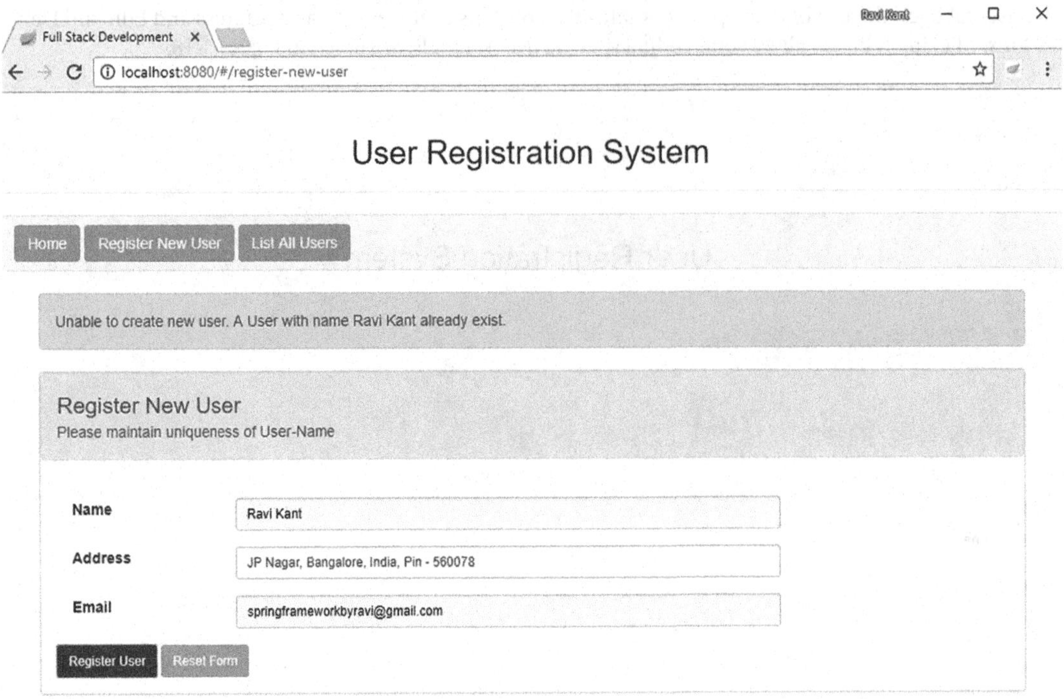

Figure 3-19. *Error message showing user already exists*

Summary

In this chapter, you looked at the concept of single-page applications. You went through the life cycle of AngularJS and saw different phases such as the bootstrap phase, the compilation phase, and the runtime data binding phase. Then you learn about AngularJS architecture concepts and the MVC architecture. You set up the AngularJS development environment by adding AngularJS to the Spring Boot application you developed in Chapter 2. You used Bootstrap for CSS designing. You saw different components of AngularJS and implemented the model, view, and controller in your application. Then you created different view pages to consume your REST API.

In the next chapter, you will implement Spring Security to secure the RESTful API that you developed using Spring Boot. Securing a web-based application is different from securing a RESTful API because in web-based applications human interaction is required from the login page to pass the user credentials. In a RESTful API, the interaction can be machine to machine or from different applications developed in different languages.

CHAPTER 4

■ ■ ■

Securing Your RESTful API Using Spring Security

In this chapter, you will secure your REST API so that only authenticated and authorized users are able to call the REST API and perform different CRUD operations. You will use Spring Security to secure your RESTful services. First I will introduce Spring Security and explain the Maven dependencies needed. Then you will learn how to implement Spring Security to secure your REST APIs in the UserRegistrationSystem application. You will also learn about the in-memory and database configuration to set up user credentials and their roles.

Introducing Spring Security

Security is the process of protecting resources from unauthenticated and unauthorized users and allowing specific (authenticated and authorized) users to access these protected resources. Security is different from firewalls, intrusion detection, JVM security, or anything else. Spring Security is primarily targeted toward Spring-based applications.

The Spring Security framework initially started as the Acegi Security framework and was later adopted by Spring as a subproject. It has become the de facto standard for securing applications developed using the Spring Framework. Spring Security supports authentication and authorization at the HTTP request method's invocation level.

Authentication and Authorization

Authentication and authorization are the two major operations provided by Spring Security (see Figure 4-1).

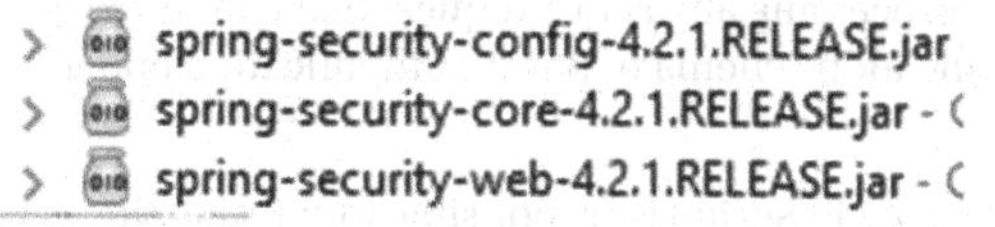

> ▸ 🗔 spring-security-config-4.2.1.RELEASE.jar
> ▸ 🗔 spring-security-core-4.2.1.RELEASE.jar - (
> ▸ 🗔 spring-security-web-4.2.1.RELEASE.jar - (

Figure 4-1. Authentication and authorization

Authentication is the process of verifying that the user is the person the user is claiming to be. Authentication takes place through identification and verification.

Authorization is the process of granting access to a resource for the authenticated user. In other words, it provides access control to an authenticated user. Let's look at an example in the UserRegistrationSystem application: the user USER can perform user registration, update user details, and get a list of users, whereas only the user ADMIN has the extra privileges to delete users. The access rights given to the client will determine the access rule for that application.

Spring Security supports URL-based security and is implemented using filters. Spring Security also supports method-level security where only authorized users are allowed to invoke specific methods granted to them.

Introducing Basic Authentication

The traditional approaches for authentication, such as using the login page and session identification, are bound to a web-based client requiring human interaction. When it comes to communicating with the REST client, which may not even be a web-based application, you need to think about the solution provided by Basic Authentication.

Basic Authentication is a standard HTTP header (Authorization) that sends Base64-encoded credentials with each request. Base64 is not encrypted or hashed in any way; in other words, the username and password are encoded in clear-text format.

The credential string contains the username and password in the format username:password. Listing 4-1 shows the algorithm used to prepare the header.

Listing 4-1. Code to Prepare the HTTP Header

```
String plain_Client_Credentials="user:password";
String base64_ClientCredentials =
new String(Base64.encodeBase64(plain_Client_Credentials.getBytes()));
HttpHeaders headers = getHeaders();
headers.add("Authorization", "Basic " + base64_ClientCredentials);
```

Listing 4-1 produces the header Authorization : Basic dXNlcjpwYXNzd29yZA==, which will be sent with each HTTP request.

Basic Authentication is one of the simplest techniques for protecting a RESTful API because it does not require cookies, a session identifier, or even a login page.

BasicAuthenticationFilter

The BasicAuthenticationFilter object is responsible for processing any HTTP request that contains an HTTP request header of Authorization with an authentication schema of Basic Authentication and a Base64-encoded username:password token.

If the authentication is successful, BasicAuthenticationFilter in Spring is responsible for putting the result (the Authentication object) into the SecurityContextHolder.

Enabling Spring Security on RESTful Services

In this section, you will understand the Spring Boot starter called Security, and then you will use it to secure your RESTful API.

What Is the Spring Boot Security Starter?

The goal of Spring Boot is to ease application development. Just like with every other feature of Spring Boot, by adding the matching starter POM, the Spring Boot starter called Security creates the basic configuration setup for the developer, including HTTP Basic Authentication and an `AuthenticationManager` bean with an in-memory default user when building an application on top of Spring Boot.

You will now configure Spring Security in your UserRegistrationSystem application. To add Spring Security to your Spring Boot application, you need to add the Spring Security dependency in the Maven pom.xml file.

Updating the pom.xml File with the Spring Security Dependency

Listing 4-2 shows the Spring Security dependency that needs to be added to pom.xml in your UserRegistrationSystem application, which will take care of all the required dependencies related to Spring Security.

Listing 4-2. Spring Security Dependency

```
<dependency>
    <groupId>org.springframework.boot</groupId>
    <artifactId>spring-boot-starter-security</artifactId>
</dependency>
```

Figure 4-2 shows the dependency added to the Maven dependency in your UserRegistrationSystem Spring Boot application.

```
2017-08-23 10:38:11.311  INFO 6372 --- [         main] b.a.s.AuthenticationManagerConfiguration :

Using default security password: 72baa813-dab9-47bf-8329-78987485785b

2017-08-23 10:38:11.425  INFO 6372 --- [         main] o.s.s.web.DefaultSecurityFilterChain      : Creating filter chain: OrRequestMatcher [r
2017-08-23 10:38:11.597  INFO 6372 --- [         main] o.s.s.web.DefaultSecurityFilterChain      : Creating filter chain: OrRequestMatcher [r
2017-08-23 10:38:11.898  INFO 6372 --- [         main] o.s.j.e.a.AnnotationMBeanExporter         : Registering beans for JMX exposure on star
2017-08-23 10:38:12.023  INFO 6372 --- [         main] s.b.c.e.t.TomcatEmbeddedServletContainer : Tomcat started on port(s): 8080 (http)
```

Figure 4-2. *Spring Security dependency*

Once you add the Spring Security dependency to the Maven pom.xml file, your entire application is protected via HTTP Basic Authentication for all resources except common static resources (CSS files, JavaScript files, and so on), and an `AuthenticationManager` bean with an in-memory default user is created for your application.

The default username is user, and the password is generated in the STS IDE console log when you run the UserRegistrationSystem application as a Spring Boot application. Once you start your Spring Boot application, you will see the generated default user's password in the logs, as follows:

```
Using default security password: 72baa813-dab9-47bf-8329-78987485785b
```

Figure 4-3 shows the log in the STS console, where you can see the default security password for your Spring Boot application.

```
INFO 9120 --- [ost-startStop-1] o.s.b.w.servlet.FilterRegistrationBean      : Mapping filter: 'characterEncodingFilter' to: [/*]
INFO 9120 --- [ost-startStop-1] o.s.b.w.servlet.FilterRegistrationBean      : Mapping filter: 'hiddenHttpMethodFilter' to: [/*]
INFO 9120 --- [ost-startStop-1] o.s.b.w.servlet.FilterRegistrationBean      : Mapping filter: 'httpPutFormContentFilter' to: [/*]
INFO 9120 --- [ost-startStop-1] o.s.b.w.servlet.FilterRegistrationBean      : Mapping filter: 'requestContextFilter' to: [/*]
INFO 9120 --- [ost-startStop-1] .s.DelegatingFilterProxyRegistrationBean    : Mapping filter: 'springSecurityFilterChain' to: [/*]
INFO 9120 --- [ost-startStop-1] o.s.b.w.servlet.ServletRegistrationBean     : Mapping servlet: 'dispatcherServlet' to [/]
```

Figure 4-3. *Generated default security password in the log*

The password generated here is random and will change every time you start your Spring Boot application, whereas the username will be always same (here it's user).

When you start your Spring Boot application after adding a Spring Security dependency, the log is printed in the console, as shown in Figure 4-4.

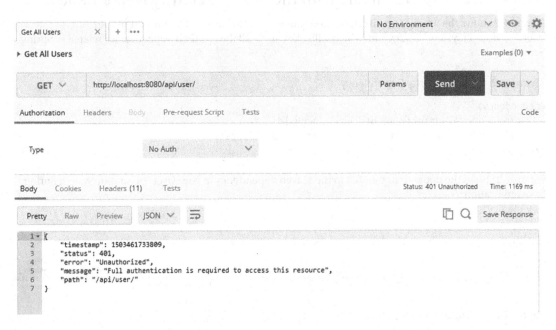

Figure 4-4. *Logging with mapping filter information*

Let's understand the magic going on behind the scenes because of autoconfiguration. The Mapping filter: 'springSecurityFilterChain' to: [/*] part shows that by default Spring Security is turned on for all URLs in the application.

Let's test your application by launching Postman and trying to call one of the REST APIs by visiting http://localhost:8080/api/user/ to get a list of users in UserRegistrationSystem. Once you hit this URL, you get a response with status 401 and the error Unauthorized stating there's been an authentication failure, as shown in Listing 4-3.

Listing 4-3. Unauthorized Error JSON Response

```
{
    "timestamp": 1503461733809,
    "status": 401,
    "error": "Unauthorized",
    "message": "Full authentication is required to access this resource",
    "path": "/api/user/"
}
```

Figure 4-5 shows the unauthorized error message with status 401, Unauthorized, in Postman.

Figure 4-5. *Unauthorized error message*

When you try to hit visit the same URL from the browser, you will get a pop-up that says "Authentication Required," as shown in Figure 4-6.

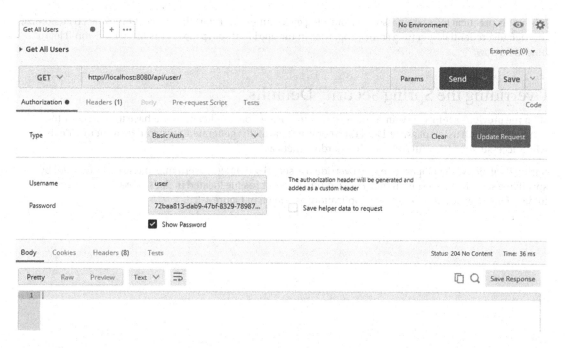

Figure 4-6. *Authentication required pop-up in browser*

You must supply a username and password along with a request to authorize. So, you will supply the username user and a password after copying the generated user's default password from the STS console to authenticate the user while accessing the RESTful API.

Launch Postman, click the Authorization tab, and then set Type as Basic Auth. Provide a username and password and click Update Request so that the request header will get a value for authorization. Finally, visit http://localhost:8080/api/user/, as shown in Figure 4-7. Since the user list is empty in the UserRegistrationSystem application, the response will show an empty list.

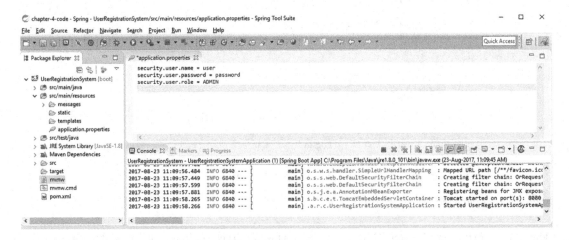

Figure 4-7. *Passing the user's credential from Postman*

It is hardly practical to copy a password from a log every time you restart the application. You can customize this default credential by setting some properties in the application.properties file, which you'll learn how to do now.

Overriding the Spring Security Defaults

With the previous setup, every time you restart your Spring Boot application, you have to search for the generated default user's password and then copy and paste this generated password to authenticate the user while accessing the RESTful API, which is hardly practical.

Spring Boot allows developers to easily override the security defaults (username, password, and role) by specifying security properties in the application.properties file located in the src\main\resources\ folder of the UserRegistrationSystem application, as shown in Figure 4-8.

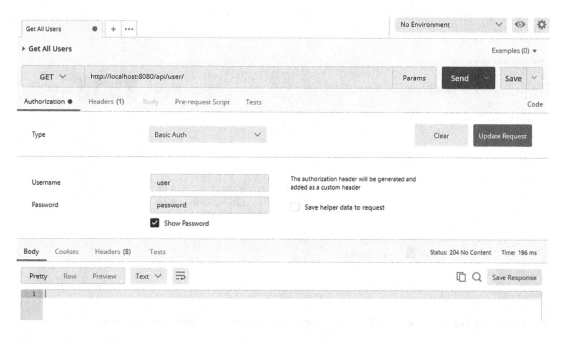

Figure 4-8. Overriding security properties in the application.properties file

Restart the UserRegistrationSystem application and observe the log in the STS console, as shown in Figure 4-6. You can clearly see that this time the Spring Boot application has not generated any default user password.

Let's test this by launching Postman and passing the user credentials, as shown in Listing 4-4.

Listing 4-4. Security Properties

```
security.user.name = user
security.user.password = password
security.user.role = ADMIN
```

While passing the user credentials from Postman in the request header, you can click Update Request in Postman to update the authorization value in the HTTP request header, as shown in Figure 4-9.

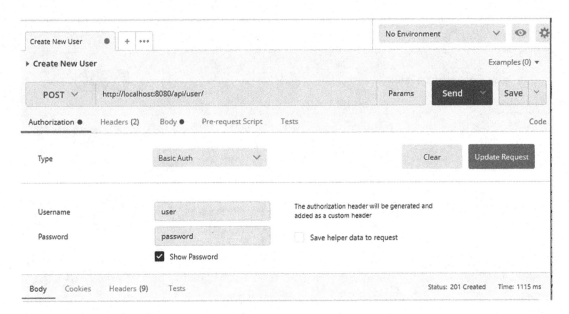

Figure 4-9. Calling the secured REST API with the newly configured username and password

Up to now you have seen lots of magic happen just by adding the dependency `spring-boot-starter-security`.

In a real-world use case, it is required that you configure more than one user with different credentials and roles to access your application. Also, it is required that you customize the users who are authorized to access your REST APIs. To achieve this, you need to bring in some Java configuration.

Customizing User Authentication

Users need to be authenticated and then authorized before being allowed to access secured resources. The authentication provider authenticates the user in Spring Security, and on successful authentication, the user is able to access secured resources from the system.

Spring Security supports multiple ways to authenticate users such as user authentication using in-memory definitions and authentication against a user repository (relational database) that is storing user details. Let's customize user authentication by configuring these users and roles:

- You will have two roles: USER and ADMIN.

- You will create one USER role with the credentials user/password.

- You will also create one ADMIN role with the credentials admin/password.

In your UserRegistrationSystem application, you will provide access for different REST endpoints to specific user roles, as shown in Table 4-1.

Table 4-1. *Mapping of APIs to User Role*

User Role	HTTP Method	API Endpoints
USER	GET	/api/user/
USER	POST	/api/user/
USER	PUT	/api/user/{id}
ADMIN	DELETE	/api/user/{id}

Authentication Customization with an In-Memory Definition

If there are only a few users for your application, you can define their details in a Spring configuration file instead of extracting user information from some persistence engine so that the user details are loaded into the application's memory. Let's create a SpringSecurityConfiguration_InMemory.java file, as shown in Listing 4-5.

Listing 4-5. Customize User Authentication in Memory

```
import org.springframework.beans.factory.annotation.Autowired;
import org.springframework.context.annotation.Configuration;
import org.springframework.http.HttpMethod;
import org.springframework.security.config.annotation.authentication.builders.
AuthenticationManagerBuilder;
import org.springframework.security.config.annotation.web.builders.HttpSecurity;
import org.springframework.security.config.annotation.web.configuration.EnableWebSecurity;
import org.springframework.security.config.annotation.web.configuration.
WebSecurityConfigurerAdapter;

@Configuration
@Order(SecurityProperties.ACCESS_OVERRIDE_ORDER)
public class SpringSecurityConfiguration_InMemory extends WebSecurityConfigurerAdapter {

        @Autowired
        protected void configureGlobal(AuthenticationManagerBuilder auth)
                    throws Exception {                      auth.inMemoryAuthentication().
                    withUser("user").password("password")
                        .roles("USER");                 auth.
                        inMemoryAuthentication().withUser("admin").
                        password("password")
                        .roles("USER", "ADMIN");
        }

        @Override
        protected void configure(HttpSecurity http) throws Exception {
```

```
        http
            .httpBasic().and()
            .authorizeRequests()
                .antMatchers(HttpMethod.GET, "/api/user/")
                    .hasRole("USER")
                .antMatchers(HttpMethod.POST, "/api/user/")
                    .hasRole("USER")
                .antMatchers(HttpMethod.PUT, "/api/user/**")
                .hasRole("USER")
                .antMatchers(HttpMethod.DELETE, "/api/user/**")
                    .hasRole("ADMIN")
                .and()
            .csrf()
                .disable();
    }
}
```

In the previous code snippet, you created a class named `SpringSecurityConfiguration_InMemory` and annotated this class with the `@Configuration` annotation, which is a Spring annotation and makes this class a configuration class. You extended this class with the `WebSecurityConfigurerAdapter` class, which allows you to configure Spring Security and override the default methods for your application.

You configured authentication by creating two users (`user` and `admin`) and their roles (`USER` and `ADMIN`) and their passwords. The `admin` user has both the `USER` and `ADMIN` roles, whereas `user` has only the `USER` role. To configure in-memory authentication, you used the `configureGlobal` method. You annotated this method with the `@Autowired` annotation. This method has an argument of type `AuthenticationManagerBuilder`.

Moving on, you overrode the second method, `configure`, which takes the argument `HttpSecurity`. In the `configure` method, you configured authorization by mapping roles to URLs. You used HTTP Basic Authentication to authenticate every request. Inside this `configure` method, you used the `anyMatchers` method to map the URL pattern and `HttpMethod` to a specific role; for example, any URL that matches `/api/user/**` and performs a `DELETE` operation should have the `ADMIN` role, and the rest can have the `USER` role. You also disabled cross-site request forgery to restrict any end user from executing unwanted actions.

Running the UserRegistrationSystem Application

Once you restart your UserRegistrationSystem application, you can test the newly implemented code by launching Postman and calling APIs along with a user's credentials.

As shown in Figure 4-10, launch Postman to register a new user in your UserRegistrationSystem application. In Postman, select the HTTP POST method and enter the URL `http://localhost:8080/api/user/`. Click the Authorization tab and select TYPE for Basic Auth. Enter the username user and password `password` and then click the Update Request button, which will update the HTTP header with the `Authorization` value. Then provide JSON data in the body (as you saw in Chapter 2), and finally click the Send button.

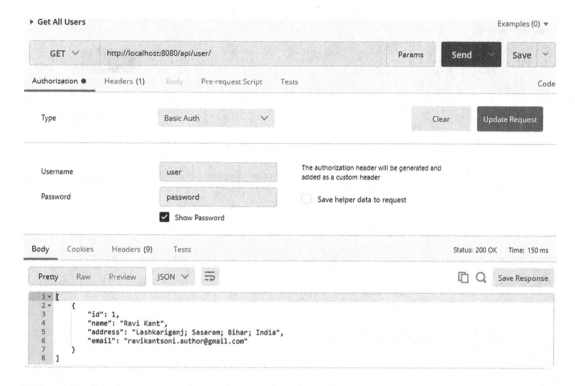

Figure 4-10. Creating a new user by passing a user's credentials

If everything goes fine, this will register a new user in your UserRegistrationSystem application.

You can call another endpoint to get a list of users. Enter the user's credentials as user/password, as shown in Figure 4-11.

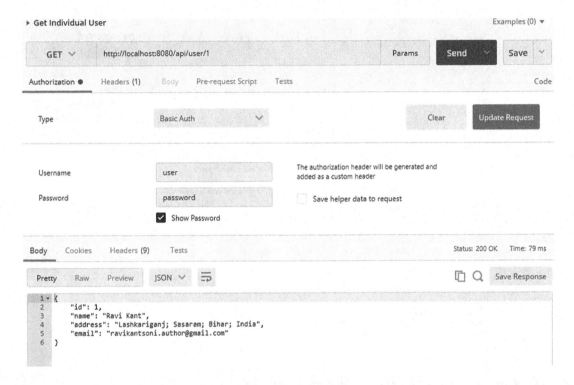

Figure 4-11. *Getting a list of users after passing a user's credential*

Similarly, you can update a user's details by calling another endpoint and passing a user's credentials as user/password, as shown in Figure 4-12.

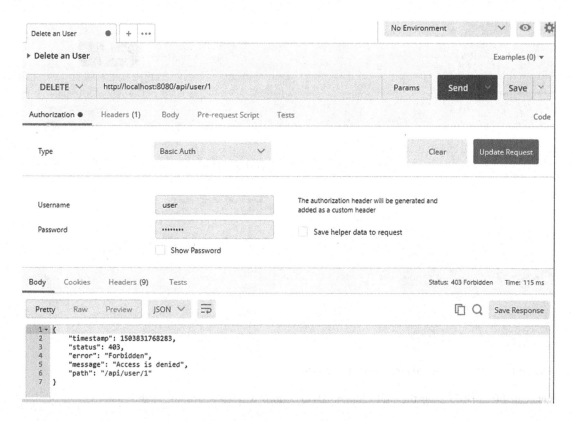

Figure 4-12. Updating a user's details by passing a user's credentials

So, you have now performed create, read, and update operations in your Spring Boot application using the user credentials of user/password. You could have also performed these operations using the admin user's credentials of admin/password because the earlier endpoints can be accessed by both of the roles USER and ADMIN.

Now, what will happen if you try to call another endpoint in your application to perform a delete operation using the USER role by passing the credentials user/password? Since you have restricted this operation for all other user roles except ADMIN, it should throw the error message "Access is denied" with status 403, Forbidden, as shown in Figure 4-13.

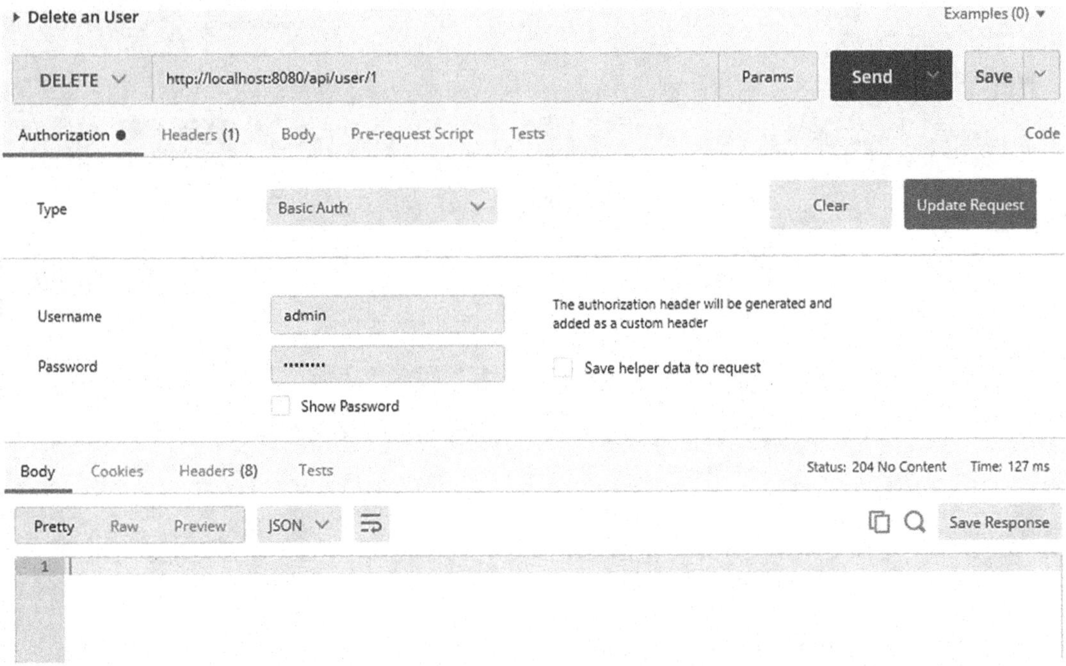

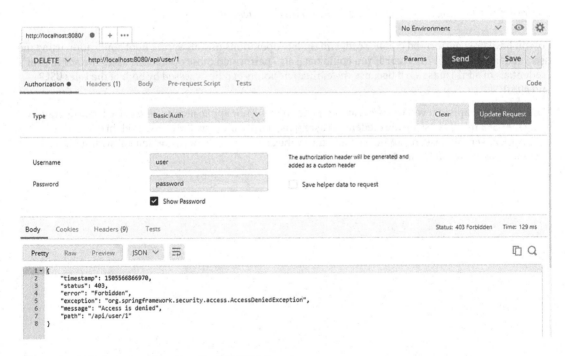

Figure 4-13. *Access is denied for unauthorized users.*

Let's call this API by passing the admin credentials to perform a delete operation, as shown in Figure 4-14.

Figure 4-14. *Delete operation using the ADMIN role*

As you have used ADMIN's credentials to call this endpoint, the operation is successful, and since this operation deleted a user from UserRegistrationSystem, the response returned an empty list.

Up to now, you have performed authentication customization with in-memory definitions. Let's take this to the next level by customizing authentication against a database.

Authentication Customization Against a Relational Database

Although you have customized Spring Security with in-memory authentication, you would like to customize the security behavior with authentication against a database so that it uses the application's users instead of generic users from Spring Boot. Let's set up the infrastructure needed for customizing authentication against a database for your UserRegistrationSystem application by creating and updating users.

Let's start by creating a UserInfo domain object, as shown in Listing 4-6. This entity class represents a UserRegistrationSystem user. The UserInfo entity class contains attributes such as the ID (userid), username, password, isEnabled, and role. You annotate this class using JPA and Hibernate annotations.

Listing 4-6. UserInfo Class

```
package com.apress.ravi.dto;

import javax.persistence.Column;
import javax.persistence.Entity;
import javax.persistence.GeneratedValue;
import javax.persistence.Id;
import javax.persistence.Table;

import org.hibernate.validator.constraints.NotEmpty;

@Entity
@Table(name = "users")
public class UserInfo {

        @Id
        @GeneratedValue
        @Column(name = "userid")
        private Long id;

        @Column(name = "username")
        @NotEmpty
        private String username;

        @Column(name = "password")
        @NotEmpty
        private String password;

        @Column(name = "enabled")
        private boolean isEnabled;

        @Column(name = "role")
        private String role;
```

```java
        public String getUsername() {
                return username;
        }

        public void setUsername(String username) {
                this.username = username;
        }

        public String getPassword() {
                return password;
        }

        public void setPassword(String password) {
                this.password = password;
        }

        public boolean isEnabled() {
                return isEnabled;
        }

        public void setEnabled(boolean isEnabled) {
                this.isEnabled = isEnabled;
        }

        public String getRole() {
                return role;
        }

        public void setRole(String role) {
                this.role = role;
        }
}
```

Since you will be storing UserRegistrationSystem's users in a database, you will require a UserInfoJpaRepository interface to perform CRUD operations on the UserInfo entity. Listing 4-7 shows the UserInfoJpaRepository interface that has extended JpaRepository. In addition to the default method provided by JpaRepository, the UserInfoJpaRepository interface contains a custom finder method named findByUsername that has a username as an argument. Spring Data JPA will provide a runtime implementation that allows the findByUsername method to return a user based on the passed-in username parameter.

Listing 4-7. UserInfoJpaRepository Interface

```java
package com.apress.ravi.repository;

import org.springframework.data.jpa.repository.JpaRepository;
import org.springframework.stereotype.Repository;

import com.apress.ravi.dto.UserInfo;
```

```
@Repository
public interface UserInfoJpaRepository extends JpaRepository<UserInfo, Long> {
        public UserInfo findByUsername(String username);
}
```

For simplicity, I have generated some test users, as shown in Listing 4-8. I have created an import.sql file in UserRegistrationSystem project's src\main\resources folder and copied these SQL statements to the end of this file. When the application gets bootstrapped, Hibernate will update the users table with these test users and make them available for the application's use.

Listing 4-8. Test User Data in the import.sql File

```
INSERT INTO users (username, password, enabled, role) VALUES ('user', 'password', true,
'USER');
INSERT INTO users (username, password, enabled, role) VALUES ('admin', 'password', true,
'ADMIN');
INSERT INTO users (username, password, enabled, role) VALUES ('ravi', 'password', true,
'USER');
```

Note that the password for the generated test user is plain text, so it is not required that you encrypt the password.

UserDetailsService Implementation

In Spring Security, UserDetailsService is used to return user information from the back end such as a database that gets compared with a submitted user's credentials during the authentication process. Listing 4-9 shows a UserDetailsService implementation for your UserRegistrationSystem application.

Listing 4-9. UserDetailsService Implementation for UserRegistrationSystem

```
package com.apress.ravi.Service;

import java.util.ArrayList;
import java.util.Collection;
import java.util.List;

import org.springframework.beans.factory.annotation.Autowired;
import org.springframework.security.core.GrantedAuthority;
import org.springframework.security.core.authority.AuthorityUtils;
import org.springframework.security.core.userdetails.UserDetails;
import org.springframework.security.core.userdetails.UserDetailsService;
import org.springframework.security.core.userdetails.UsernameNotFoundException;
import org.springframework.stereotype.Service;

import com.apress.ravi.dto.UserInfo;
import com.apress.ravi.repository.UserInfoJpaRepository;
```

```
@Service
public class UserInfoDetailsService implements UserDetailsService {

        @Autowired
        private UserInfoJpaRepository userInfoJpaRepository;

        @Override
        public UserDetails loadUserByUsername(String username)
                        throws UsernameNotFoundException {

                UserInfo user = userInfoJpaRepository.findByUsername(username);
                if (user == null) {
                        throw new UsernameNotFoundException(
                                "Opps! user not found with user-name: " + username);
                }

                return new org.springframework.security.core.userdetails.User(
                                user.getUsername(), user.getPassword(),
                                getAuthorities(user));
        }

        private Collection<GrantedAuthority> getAuthorities(UserInfo user) {
                List<GrantedAuthority> authorities = new ArrayList<>();
                authorities = AuthorityUtils.createAuthorityList(user.getRole());
                return authorities;
        }
}
```

The UserInfoDetailsService class autowired UserInfoJpaRepository to retrieve UserInfo details from the database. This class overrides the loadUserByUsername method that returns an instance of type UserDetails. This method first checks whether the user retrieved from the database is null and, if so, throws a UsernameNotFoundException exception with an appropriate message. If the retrieved user is not null, then this method creates an instance of org.springframework.security.core.userdetails.User and populates it with the user data returned from the database.

Customizing Spring Security and Securing the URI

Now you will be customizing Spring Security's default behavior and securing a URI by creating a SpringSecurityConfiguration_Database configuration class that is annotated with the @Configuration and @EnableWebSecurity annotations. This configuration class extends the org.springframework. security.config.annotation.web.configuration.WebSecurityConfigurerAdapter class that provides a helper method to configure Spring Security. Listing 4-10 shows the SpringSecurityConfiguration database that contains the Spring Security configuration for the UserRegistrationSystem application.

Listing 4-10. Security Configuration for UserRegistrationSystem

```
package com.apress.ravi.Security;

import org.springframework.beans.factory.annotation.Autowired;
import org.springframework.context.annotation.Configuration;
```

```
import org.springframework.security.config.annotation.authentication.builders.
AuthenticationManagerBuilder;
import org.springframework.security.config.annotation.web.builders.HttpSecurity;
import org.springframework.security.config.annotation.web.configuration.EnableWebSecurity;
import org.springframework.security.config.annotation.web.configuration.
WebSecurityConfigurerAdapter;
import org.springframework.security.config.http.SessionCreationPolicy;

import com.apress.ravi.Service.UserInfoDetailsService;

@Configuration
@EnableWebSecurity
public class SpringSecurityConfiguration_Database
            extends WebSecurityConfigurerAdapter {

    @Autowired
    private UserInfoDetailsService userInfoDetailsService;

    @Override
    protected void configure(
                AuthenticationManagerBuilder authenticationManagerBuilder)
                throws Exception {

        authenticationManagerBuilder
                .userDetailsService(userInfoDetailsService);
    }

    @Override
    protected void configure(HttpSecurity http) throws Exception {

        http.sessionManagement()
                .sessionCreationPolicy(SessionCreationPolicy.STATELESS)
                .and()
                .authorizeRequests()
                        .antMatchers("/api/user/**")
                        .authenticated()
                .and()
                .httpBasic()
                        .realmName("User Registration System")
                .and()
                .csrf()
                        .disable();
    }
}
```

The SpringSecurityConfiguration_Database configuration class has autowired the
UserInfoDetailsService bean. This configuration class has overridden WebSecurityConfigurerAdapter's
configure method, which takes AuthenticationManagerBuilder as a parameter. AuthenticationManager
Builder is a helper class that implements the Builder pattern and provides a way of assembling an
AuthenticationManager. You have used AuthenticationManagerBuilder in this method to add the
UserInfoDetailsService instance.

Also, you overrode another `WebSecurityConfigurerAdapter`'s configure method in the `SpringSecurityConfiguration` database configuration class, which helps in configuring HTTP Basic Authentication to use the UserRegistrationSystem user. This configuration secures all endpoints and requires authentication to access resources. This method takes `HttpSecurity` as an argument, which allows you to specify those URIs that should be secured or unsecured. The implementation of this method begins with requesting Spring Security to not create an HTTP session and not store logged-in users' `SecurityContext` values in the session, which you have achieved using the `SessionCreationPolicy.STATELESS` creation policy. Then you used `antMatchers` to provide an Ant-style URI expression that you want Spring Security protecting using the authenticated method, which allows an authenticated user to access the respective endpoint. Finally, you enabled HTTP Basic Authentication and also set the realm name to User Registration System.

In addition, you disabled CSRF for HTTP methods to keep things simple. CSRF is a type of security vulnerability whereby a malicious web site forces users to execute unwanted commands on another web site in which they are currently authenticated. By default, Spring Security enables CSRF protection and is highly recommended when requests are submitted by a user via a browser. For services (REST) that are used by nonbrowser clients, CSRF can be disabled.

Method-Level Security

Method-level security is an alternate to secure URI access. Sometimes it is required to ensure that only users with administrative privileges (having the `admin` role) can delete a registered user in UserRegistrationSystem, which can be achieved by enforcing fine-grained security control on methods. You will be applying Spring Security's method-level security on the `deleteUser` method.

To enable Spring's method-level security, annotate the `SpringSecurityConfiguration_Database` configuration class with the `org.springframework.security.config.annotation.method.configuration.EnableGlobalMethodSecurity` annotation, as shown in Listing 4-11.

Listing 4-11. Adding the EnableGlobalMethodSecurity Annotation

```
package com.apress.ravi.Security;

import org.springframework.beans.factory.annotation.Autowired;
import org.springframework.context.annotation.Configuration;
import org.springframework.security.config.annotation.authentication.builders.
AuthenticationManagerBuilder;
import org.springframework.security.config.annotation.method.configuration.
EnableGlobalMethodSecurity;
import org.springframework.security.config.annotation.web.builders.HttpSecurity;
import org.springframework.security.config.annotation.web.configuration.EnableWebSecurity;
import org.springframework.security.config.annotation.web.configuration.
WebSecurityConfigurerAdapter;
import org.springframework.security.config.http.SessionCreationPolicy;

import com.apress.ravi.chapter2.Service.UserInfoDetailsService;

@Configuration
@EnableWebSecurity
@EnableGlobalMethodSecurity(prePostEnabled = true)
public class SpringSecurityConfiguration_Database
                extends WebSecurityConfigurerAdapter {

        //...code
}
```

Spring Security supports a rich set of method-level authorization annotations along with class-level authorization annotations. You set the prePostEnabled flag to true in EnableGlobalMethodSecurity, which enables the Spring Security annotation to perform pre- and post-method invocation authorization checks. So, annotate the UserRegistrationRestController's deleteUser method with the @PreAuthorize annotation, as shown in Listing 4-12.

Listing 4-12. Adding the PreAuthorize Annotation

```
import org.springframework.security.access.prepost.PreAuthorize;

@DeleteMapping("/{id}")
@PreAuthorize("hasAuthority('ADMIN')")
public ResponseEntity<UsersDTO> deleteUser(@PathVariable("id") final Long id) {

        //...code
}
```

The @PreAuthorize annotation only allows an authorized user to invoke the deleteUser method. hasAuthority checks whether the logged-in user has ADMIN authority and lets Spring Security make the decision.

Restart the UserRegistrationSystem application and launch Postman to perform a DELETE on the endpoint http://localhost:8080/api/user/1. Set the Authorization type in Postman to Basic Auth and enter a username of user and a password of password, which has the role USER. Since user doesn't have administrative rights, an unauthorized response with the message "Access is denied" will be returned, as shown in Figure 4-15.

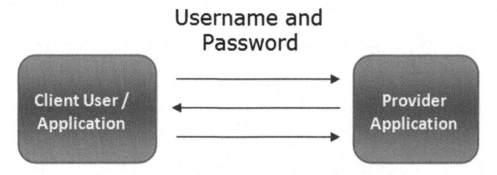

Figure 4-15. Unauthorized delete response

Summary

In this chapter, you were introduced to Spring Security and the concepts of authentication and authorization. You enabled Spring Security on RESTful services by implementing Basic Authentication. Then you customized the authentication with in-memory databases and against databases. In the next chapter, you will explore how to consume a secured RESTful API using AngularJS.

CHAPTER 5

■ ■ ■

Consuming Secured RESTful Services Using AngularJS

In Chapter 2, you created a REST application called UserRegistrationSystem using Spring Boot and performed CRUD operations. In Chapter 3, you created a single-page application (SPA) using AngularJS and consumed the REST endpoints. In Chapter 4, you secured your REST endpoints using Spring Security.

In this chapter, I will show you how Spring Boot, Spring Security, and AngularJS can work together to provide a pleasant and secure user experience. You will consume secure RESTful services using AngularJS. You will initially start by sending an authorization header with each request in AngularJS. Then you will create a login page and update the Spring Security configuration to support the login and logout authentication process.

Enabling Basic Authentication in Spring Security

In Chapter 4, you secured the UserRegistrationSystem application's REST endpoint with Basic Authentication just by updating the Maven pom.xml file with the Spring Boot starter Security dependency and by adding the Spring Security configuration file with an in-memory authentication configuration, as shown in Listing 5-1.

Listing 5-1. In-Memory Authentication Configuration

```
@Configuration
@Order(SecurityProperties.ACCESS_OVERRIDE_ORDER)
public class SpringSecurityConfiguration_InMemory
            extends WebSecurityConfigurerAdapter {

    @Autowired
    protected void configureGlobal(AuthenticationManagerBuilder auth)
                throws Exception {
        auth.inMemoryAuthentication()
                .withUser("admin").password("password")
                    .roles("USER", "ADMIN");
    }

    @Override
    protected void configure(HttpSecurity http) throws Exception {
```

© Ravi Kant Soni 2017
R. K. Soni, *Full Stack AngularJS for Java Developers*, https://doi.org/10.1007/978-1-4842-3198-2_5

```
        http
                .httpBasic()
                        .realmName("User Registration System")
                .and()
                .authorizeRequests()
                        .antMatchers(HttpMethod.GET, "/api/user/")
                                .hasRole("USER")
                        .antMatchers(HttpMethod.POST, "/api/user/")
                                .hasRole("USER")
                        .antMatchers(HttpMethod.PUT, "/api/user/**")
                                .hasRole("USER")
                        .antMatchers(HttpMethod.DELETE, "/api/user/**")
                                .hasRole("ADMIN")
                .and()
                .csrf()
                        .disable();
        }
}
```

In Chapter 3, you developed UserRegistrationSystem as an SPA using AngularJS to consume a REST endpoint. With the Spring Security configuration, now when you try to access your page using the URL http://localhost:8080/#/list-all-users in a browser, an "Authentication Required" pop-up will appear, and you will need to enter a username and password that you have configured in the security configuration file in order to access the /list-all-users page, as shown in Figure 5-1.

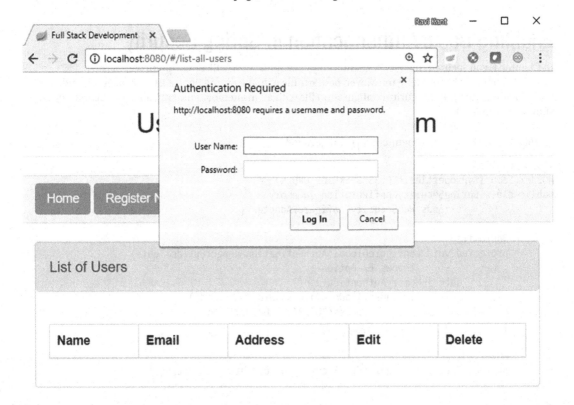

Figure 5-1. Authentication required to access a page in the browser

The issue with is that every time you open a browser and access a web page, a pop-up appears in the browser for a username and password. You can fix this issue by sending an authorization header with each request in AngularJS.

Sending an Authorization Header with Each Request in AngularJS

Basic Authentication allows a client to send its Base64-encoded credentials using an authorization header in each HTTP request. That means each request is independent of other requests, and the server doesn't maintain any state information for the client.

As you have to send an authentication header with each request, an HTTP interceptor is a good choice to handle it instead of manually specifying the authentication header in all $http methods.

Adding the HTTP Interceptor in AngularJS

When a request/response communicate over an HTTP call and you want to inject some custom logic, then an HTTP interceptor comes into the picture. An HTTP interceptor always executes custom logic for authenticating, authorizing, managing session state, logging, modifying a response, rewriting URLs, handling errors, caching, adding custom headers, adding a timestamp in the request/response, and encrypting and decrypting the request and response information before and after the HTTP call, as shown in Figure 5-2.

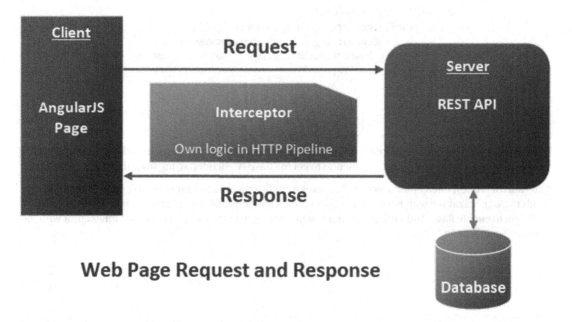

Figure 5-2. *HTTP interceptor*

AngularJS supports four kinds of HTTP interceptor: request, response, requestError, and responseError.

- The request interceptor is called before $http sends the request to the server. The request function takes the config object as an input parameter and returns a config object after adding, modifying, or removing data to or from this object.

- The response interceptor is called after $http receives the response from the server. The response function takes a response object as a parameter and modifies the response data or adds a new set of values, calling another module or service call before returning a response object.

- The requestError interceptor gets called when any error is thrown by the request interceptor.

- The responseError interceptor gets called when any call to a server has failed and the application needs to trigger some action based on different HTTP status codes.

Let's implements the HTTP interceptor in your UserRegistrationSystem application.

authInterceptor.js

Create an interceptor named AuthInterceptor in the authInterceptor.js file, as shown in Listing 5-2.

Listing 5-2. HTTP Interceptor with Request Function

```
app.factory('AuthInterceptor', [ function() {
        return {
                'request' : function(config) {
                        config.headers = config.headers || {};
                        var encodedString = btoa("admin:password");
                        config.headers.Authorization = 'Basic ' + encodedString;
                        return config;
                }
        };
} ]);
```

In Listing 5-1, you configured security authentication credentials with the username admin and the password password. Also, you called the btoa() function to get the Base64-encoded string from the user's credentials.

You called a request interceptor function that takes a config object as a parameter. You updated config. headers.Authorization with Basic Authentication data and returned this updated config object. This is sufficient to enable Basic Authentication. You just need to register the AuthInterceptor interceptor with the AngularJS application.

Updating app.js

To register the `AuthInterceptor` interceptor with the AngularJS application, you need to update the `app.js` file, as shown in Listing 5-3.

Listing 5-3. Registering the Interceptor in the Application by Updating app.js

```
var app = angular.module('userregistrationsystem', [ 'ngRoute', 'ngResource' ]);

app.config(function($routeProvider) {
        $routeProvider.when('/list-all-users', {
                templateUrl : '/template/listuser.html',
                controller : 'listUserController'
        }).when('/register-new-user',{
                templateUrl : '/template/userregistration.html',
                controller : 'registerUserController'
        }).when('/update-user/:id',{
                templateUrl : '/template/userupdation.html' ,
                controller : 'usersDetailsController'
        }).otherwise({
                redirectTo : '/home',
                templateUrl : '/template/home.html',
        });
});

app.config(['$httpProvider', function($httpProvider) {
  $httpProvider.interceptors.push('AuthInterceptor');
}]);
```

In Listing 5-3, you registered the `AuthInterceptor` interceptor (interceptors are service factories) with `$httpProvider` just by adding them to the `$httpProvider.interceptors` array using the push method. This service factory is called and returns the interceptor.

Updating index.html

Now you need to update the `index.html` file to include the `authInterceptor.js` file in your application, as shown in Listing 5-4.

Listing 5-4. Updating the index.html File

```
<!DOCTYPE html>
<html lang="en" ng-app="userregistrationsystem">
<head>
<title>Full Stack Development</title>
<link rel="stylesheet" href="/css/app.css">
</head>
<body>
        <div class="page-header text-center">
                <h2>User Registration System</h2>
        </div>
```

```
<nav class="navbar navbar-default">
        <div class="container-fluid">
                <a href="#/"
                        class="btn btn-info navbar-btn"
                        role="button">
                                Home
                </a>
                <a href="#/register-new-user"
                        class="btn btn-info navbar-btn"
                        role="button">
                                Register New User
                </a>
                <a href="#/list-all-users"
                        class="btn btn-info"
                        role="button">
                                List All Users
                </a>
        </div>
</nav>
<div ng-view></div>
<script src="/webjars/angularjs/1.4.9/angular.js"></script>
<script src="/webjars/angularjs/1.4.9/angular-resource.js"></script>
<script src="/webjars/angularjs/1.4.9/angular-route.js"></script>
<script src="/js/app.js"></script>
<script src="/js/controller.js"></script>
<script src="/js/authInterceptor.js"></script>
<link rel="stylesheet"href="/webjars/bootstrap/3.3.6/css/bootstrap.css">
</body>
</html>
```

Running the Application

Let's restart the UserRegistrationSystem application and visit the URL http://localhost:8080/#/list-all-users in the browser. The list-all-users page will display in the browser without displaying any pop-up for authentication, as shown in Figure 5-3.

Figure 5-3. *The list-all-users page displaying in the browser*

HTTP Request with Basic Authentication Header: Verify in Developer Tools

You can verify the HTTP request that the Basic Authentication header sent while requesting the URL
http://localhost:8080/#/list-all-users. Open Developer Tools in the browser (here, it's a Chrome
browser), select Network, and click the Headers tab to monitor the request headers with authorization data,
as shown in Figure 5-4.

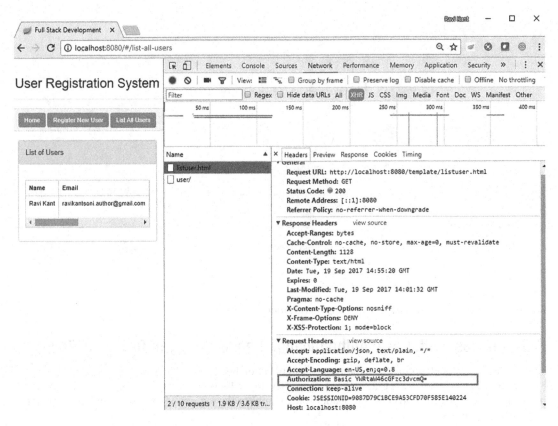

Figure 5-4. *Monitoring Basic Authentication header in Developer Tools*

So far, you have successfully sent an authorization header with each request using the interceptor, and you were able to consume a secured REST endpoint. You have configured a single user in the AngularJS interceptor to perform Basic Authentication. An issue will arise when you have more than one user with different roles. To address this issue, you need to have a login page where you can enter a username and password to get authenticated and authorized before accessing any resource, and you need to have a Logout button on the web page.

In the next section, you will create a login page and perform the login and logout authentication process. You will be using form-based authentication in your UserRegistrationSystem application, which will provide more flexibility than HTTP Basic Authentication.

The Login Page

In this section, you will be using AngularJS to authenticate a user via a login form and fetch a secured resource to render JSON data in the UI. This login form gives the user some control over whether to authenticate.

Updating index.html: Adding Navigation to the Welcome Page

As you saw in Chapter 3, index.html is the core of an SPA, and you already have a really basic one so far. You need to offer some more navigation features such as login and logout capabilities. So, let's modify your existing src/main/resources/static/index.html file, as shown in Listing 5-5.

Listing 5-5. Updating src/main/resources/static/index.html

```
<!DOCTYPE html>
<html lang="en" ng-app="userregistrationsystem">
<head>
<title>Full Stack Development</title>
<link rel="stylesheet" href="/css/app.css">
</head>
<body>
        <div class="page-header text-center">
                <h2>User Registration System</h2>
        </div>
        <nav class="navbar navbar-default">
                <div class="container-fluid">
                        <div class="container-fluid" ng-show="!authenticated">
                                <a href="#/login"
                                        class="btn btn-info navbar-btn"
                                        role="button">
                                                Login
                                </a>
                        <p>Login to go to Home Page</p>
                        </div>
                        <div ng-show="authenticated">
                                <a href="#/"
                                        class="btn btn-info navbar-btn"
                                        role="button">
                                                Home
                                </a>
                                <a href="#/register-new-user"
                                        class="btn btn-info navbar-btn"
                                        role="button">
                                                Register New User
                                </a>
                                <a href="#/list-all-users"
                                        class="btn btn-info"
                                        role="button">
                                                List All Users
                                </a>
                                <a href="#/logout"
                                        class="btn btn-danger navbar-btn pull-right"
                                        role="button">
                                                Logout
                                </a>
                        </div>
                </div>
        </nav>
```

```
<div ng-view></div>
<script src="/webjars/angularjs/1.4.9/angular.js"></script>
<script src="/webjars/angularjs/1.4.9/angular-resource.js"></script>
<script src="/webjars/angularjs/1.4.9/angular-route.js"></script>
<script src="/js/app.js"></script>
<script src="/js/controller.js"></script>
<link rel="stylesheet"
        href="/webjars/bootstrap/3.3.6/css/bootstrap.css">
</body>
</html>
```

As shown in Listing 5-5, the updated index.html is not that different from the original one. You added a new div containing an anchor tag for login. And you added an anchor tag for logout. You used AngularJS's ng-show to hide/show elements on the page based on authenticated.

Updating app.js: Adding Navigation to the Angular Application

You now need to update the UserRegistrationSystem application (in src/main/resources/static/js/app.js) to add new navigation features for logging in and logging out, as shown in Listing 5-6.

Listing 5-6. Updating src/main/resources/static/js/app.js

```
var app = angular.module('userregistrationsystem', [ 'ngRoute', 'ngResource' ]);

app.config(function($routeProvider, $locationProvider) {
        $routeProvider
                .when('/', {
                        templateUrl : '/template/home.html',
                        controller : 'homeController'
                })

                .when('/list-all-users', {
                        templateUrl : '/template/listuser.html',
                        controller : 'listUserController'
                })

                .when('/register-new-user',{
                        templateUrl : '/template/userregistration.html',
                        controller : 'registerUserController'
                })

                .when('/update-user/:id',{
                        templateUrl : '/template/userupdation.html' ,
                        controller : 'usersDetailsController'
                })

                .when('/login',{
                        templateUrl : '/login/login.html',
                        controller : 'loginController'
                })
```

```
        .when('/logout',{
                templateUrl : '/login/login.html',
                controller : 'logoutController'
        })

        .otherwise({
                redirectTo : '/login'
        });
});

app.config(['$httpProvider', function($httpProvider) {
        $httpProvider.defaults.headers.common["X-Requested-With"] = 'XMLHttpRequest';
}]);
```

In Listing 5-4, you added the homeController controller for the link /. You also set up new links such as /
login and /logout and their templateUrl and controller.

The custom X-Requested-With line is a conventional header sent by browser clients. Spring Security
responds to it by not sending a WWW-Authenticate header in a 401 response, and thus the browser will not
open an authentication pop-up dialog, which is desirable in your UserRegistrationSystem application since
you want to control the authentication.

Creating login.html: The Login Form

Let's create a login form that goes in src/main/resources/static/login/login.html, as shown in Listing 5-7.

Listing 5-7. src/main/resources/static/login/login.html

```
<div class="container-fluid">
 <div class="container">
  <div class="panel panel-default ">
   <div class="alert alert-success">
    <span class="lead">Login Page</span>
    <p>Enter Username and Password</p>
    <br/>
    <div class="alert alert-danger" ng-show="loginerror">
      There was a problem logging in. Please try again.
    </div>
   </div>
   <div class="panel-body ">
    <div class="container">
     <form ng-submit="loginUser()" name="myForm"
       class="form-horizontal">
      <div class="row">
        <div class="form-group col-md-12">
          <label class="col-md-2 control-lable" for="uname"> Username
          </label>
          <div class="col-md-7">
            <input type="text" ng-model="credentials.username" id="uname"
                class="form-control input-sm" placeholder="Enter Username" />
          </div>
        </div>
      </div>
```

```
      </div>
      <div class="row">
        <div class="form-group col-md-12">
          <label class="col-md-2 control-lable" for="password">
              Password
          </label>
          <div class="col-md-7">
            <input type="password" ng-model="credentials.password"
            id="password" class="form-control input-sm" placeholder="Enter Password" />
          </div>
        </div>
      </div>
      <div class="row">
        <div class="form-actions floatRight">
          <input type="submit" value="Login" class="btn btn-primary btn-sm">
          <button type="button" ng-click="resetForm()" class="btn btn-warning
          btn-sm">Reset Form</button>
        </div>
      </div>
    </form>
    </div>
  </div>
 </div>
</div>
</div>
```

As shown in Listing 5-5, this is a simple and standard login form; it contains two fields for entering the username and password and two buttons for logging in (submitting the form via ng-submit) and resetting the form, as shown in Figure 5-5.

Figure 5-5. *Login form with input boxes and buttons*

The login form control uses ng-model to pass data between the HTML (login.html) and the Angular controller (controller.js), and in this case you are using a credentials object to hold the username and password. You also added code to show an error message when the Angular model contains a loginerror value, as shown in Figure 5-6.

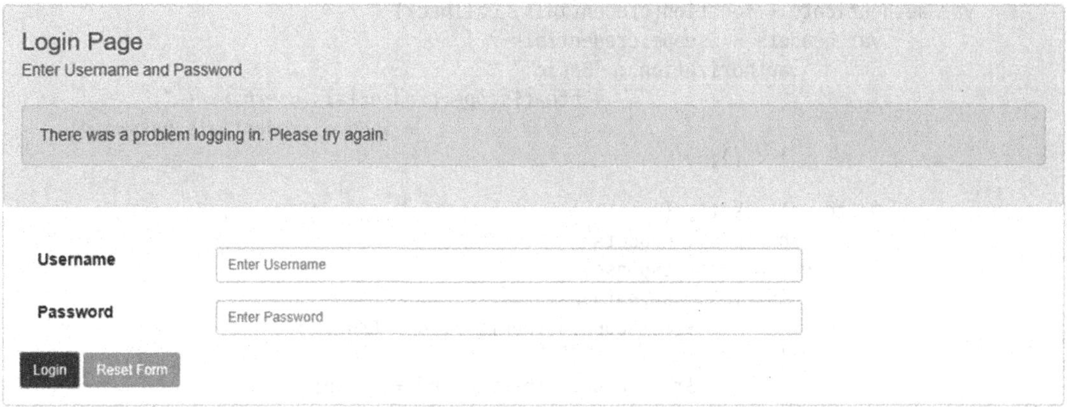

Figure 5-6. *Login page with error message*

As per the routes defined in an application, such as app.js, you have defined a login form that needs to be linked with loginController, so let's update your controller.js file.

Updating controller.js for the Login and Logout Authentication Process

To support the login and logout authentication process, you need to add some more features. You need to add three new controllers: homeController, loginController, and logoutController. You add these to the existing UserRegistrationSystem application in the src/main/resources/static/js/controller.js file, as shown in Listing 5-8.

Listing 5-8. src/main/resources/static/js/controller.js

```
app.controller('homeController', function($rootScope, $scope,
             $http, $location, $route){

        if ($rootScope.authenticated) {
                $location.path("/");
                $scope.loginerror = false;
        } else {
                $location.path("/login");
                $scope.loginerror = true;
        }
});

app.controller('loginController', function($rootScope, $scope,
             $http, $location, $route){
        $scope.credentials = {};

        $scope.resetForm = function() {
                $scope.credentials = null;
        }
```

```
        var authenticate = function(credentials, callback) {
                var headers = $scope.credentials ? {
                        authorization : "Basic "
                                        + btoa($scope.credentials.username + ":"
                                                        + $scope.credentials.password)
                        } : {};

                $http.get('user', {
                        headers : headers
                }).then(function(response) {
                        if (response.data.name) {
                                $rootScope.authenticated = true;
                        } else {
                                $rootScope.authenticated = false;
                        }
                        callback && callback();
                }, function() {
                        $rootScope.authenticated = false;
                        callback && callback();
                });
        }

        authenticate();

        $scope.loginUser = function() {
                authenticate($scope.credentials, function() {
                    if ($rootScope.authenticated) {
                      $location.path("/");
                      $scope.loginerror = false;
                    } else {
                      $location.path("/login");
                      $scope.loginerror = true;
                    }
                });
        };
});

app.controller('logoutController', function($rootScope, $scope,
            $http, $location, $route){
        $http.post('logout', {}).finally(function() {
            $rootScope.authenticated = false;
            $location.path("/");
        });
});
```

As shown in Listing 5-8, you created new controllers named homeController, loginController, and logoutController. The homeController controller checks whether authenticated inside $rootScope is true and then sets $location.path with / and loginerror in $scopeto to false, or it sets $location.path with /login and loginerror in $scope to true.

The loginController controller will be executed when the login page loads. This controller starts with initializing the credentials object, and then it defines the functions: the resetForm() method that resets the input box for the username and password with a null value, the authenticate() function (a local helper function) that loads a user resource from the back end, and the function loginUser() that you need in the form.

The local helper function authenticate() is called when the controller is loaded to see whether the user is actually already authenticated, and you need this function just to make a remote call because the actual authentication is done by the server. This function also sets an application-wide flag called authenticated that you used in the index.html page to show/hide elements and control which parts of the page are rendered. You achieved this application-wide flag using $rootScope because it's convenient and easy to follow, and you need to share the authenticated flag between different controllers.

This authenticate() method makes a GET call to a relative resource called /user. While calling from the loginUser() function, the authenticate() function adds the Base64-encoded credentials in the request headers, so on the server it does an authentication and accepts a cookie in return. The loginUser() function also sets a local $scope.loginerror flag accordingly when it gets the result of the authentication that is being used to control the display of the error message in the login page.

If the user is authenticated, then you show a Logout button on each web page. Clicking the Logout button will let logoutController to be executed. The logoutController controller sends an HTTP POST to /logout, which you do not need to implement on the server because it is added for you already by Spring Security. To add more control over the default behavior of the logout process provided by Spring Security, you could use the HttpSecurity callback's inSpringSecurityConfiguration in Memory.java to, for instance, execute some business logic after logout.

Updating the Back-End Code

You also need to update your back-end code to support the login and logout authentication process in your UserRegistrationSystem application.

Creating a New RESTful Endpoint to Get the Currently Authenticated User

As you saw in Listing 5-8, the authenticate() function makes a GET request to the resource /user to get the currently authenticated user. So, to service the authenticate() function, you have to add a new REST endpoint in your UserRegistrationSystem application. Let's create the ServiceAuthenticate.java class inside the package com.apress.ravi.Rest under the src/main/java folder, as shown in Listing 5-9.

Listing 5-9. com.apress.ravi.Rest.ServiceAuthenticate.java

```
package com.apress.ravi.Rest;

import java.security.Principal;

import org.springframework.web.bind.annotation.RequestMapping;
import org.springframework.web.bind.annotation.RestController;

@RestController
public class ServiceAuthenticate {

        @RequestMapping("/user")
        public Principal user(Principal user) {
                return user;
        }
}
```

If the /user resource is reachable, then it will return the authenticated user.

Updating the Spring Security Configuration to Handle Login Requests

You also need to update your existing Spring Security configuration file com.apress.ravi.Security. SpringSecurityConfiguration_InMemory.java, as shown in Listing 5-10.

Listing 5-10. SpringSecurityConfiguration_InMemory.java

```
package com.apress.ravi.Security;

import org.springframework.beans.factory.annotation.Autowired;
import org.springframework.boot.autoconfigure.security.SecurityProperties;
import org.springframework.context.annotation.Configuration;
import org.springframework.core.annotation.Order;
import org.springframework.security.config.annotation.authentication.builders.
AuthenticationManagerBuilder;
import org.springframework.security.config.annotation.web.builders.HttpSecurity;
import org.springframework.security.config.annotation.web.configuration.
WebSecurityConfigurerAdapter;
import org.springframework.security.web.csrf.CookieCsrfTokenRepository;

@Configuration
@Order(SecurityProperties.ACCESS_OVERRIDE_ORDER)
public class SpringSecurityConfiguration_InMemory
                extends WebSecurityConfigurerAdapter {

        @Autowired
        protected void configureGlobal(AuthenticationManagerBuilder auth)
                        throws Exception {
                auth.inMemoryAuthentication().
                        withUser("user").password("password")
                                .roles("USER");
                auth.inMemoryAuthentication()
                        .withUser("admin").password("password")
                                .roles("USER", "ADMIN");
        }

        @Override
        protected void configure(HttpSecurity http) throws Exception {

                http
                        .httpBasic()
                                .realmName("User Registration System")
                        .and()
                        .authorizeRequests()
                                .antMatchers("/login/login.html", "/template/home.html",
                                "/").permitAll()
                                .anyRequest().authenticated()
                                .and()
                                .csrf()
.csrfTokenRepository(CookieCsrfTokenRepository.withHttpOnlyFalse());
        }
}
```

In Listing 5-10, you updated your existing `configure` method to handle the login request. You allowed anonymous access to the static resources such as `/login/login.html`, `/template/home.html`, and `/`, because these HTML resources need to be available to anonymous users.

Spring Security provides a special `CsrfTokenRepository` to send a cookie. When you start with a clean browser (Ctrl+F5 or incognito in Chrome), the first request to the server has no cookies, but the server sends back `Set-Cookie` for `JSESSIONID` (the regular `HttpSession`) and `X-XSRF-TOKEN`, which are the CRSF cookies that you set up in Listing 5-10. Subsequent requests will have these cookies, which are important: the Spring Security application doesn't work without them, and they are providing some really basic security features (authentication and CSRF protection). When you log out, the values of the cookies change. Spring Security expects the token sent to it in a header called `X-CSRF`. From the initial request that loads the home page, the value of the CSRF token was available in the `HttpRequest` attributes on the server side. Angular has built-in support for CSRF (which it calls XSRF) based on cookies. Angular wants the cookie name to be `XSRF-TOKEN`, and the best part of Spring Security is that it provides it as a request attribute by default.

Running the Application

Let's restart your UserRegistrationSystem application to test these features. Open a browser and visit `http://localhost:8080/`, and your application will redirect to the link `http://localhost:8080/#/login` to provide a login page, as shown in Figure 5-7.

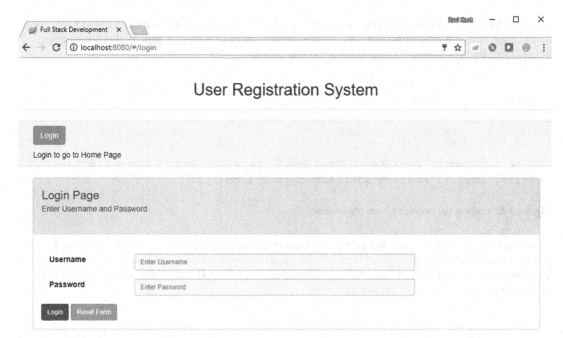

Figure 5-7. *Navigating to the login page*

On successful login, after entering the username and password and clicking the Login button, you will be redirected to the home page, as shown in Figure 5-8.

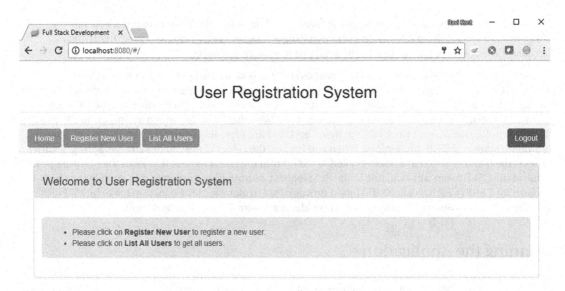

Figure 5-8. *Navigating to the home page after logging in to the application*

Once you have logged in to your application, you can directly call an endpoint from the same browser. Let's open a new tab in the same browser where you performed a successful login to your application and visit http://localhost:8080/api/user/, as shown in Figure 5-9.

```
[{"id":1,"name":"Ravi Kant","address":"Lashkariganj; Sasaram; Bihar;
India","email":"ravikantsoni.author@gmail.com"}]
```

Figure 5-9. *Calling the endpoint from the browser*

Once you click the Logout button from the web page (other than the login page after successful login), you will be redirected to the login page. To verify whether you have successfully logged out from the application, try calling the endpoint from the same browser by visiting http://localhost:8080/api/user/. You will be prompted with a pop-up, as shown in Figure 5-10.

Figure 5-10. *Authentication pop-up opening once a user is logged out and tries to call the endpoint*

Summary

In this chapter, you successfully consumed a secure RESTful service using AngularJS. You started by enabling Basic Authentication in Spring Security. Then you sent an authorization header with each request. Finally, you created a login page to perform the login/logout authentication process.

In the next chapter, you will build a RESTful client and test the RESTful services.

CHAPTER 6

■ ■ ■

Building a RESTful Client and Testing RESTful Services

In Chapter 2, you built RESTful services using Spring Boot. You created different endpoints to perform CRUD operations in your UserRegistrationSystem application. You have already used Postman (from Chrome) to see all the HTTP methods in action.

In this chapter, you will be building a REST client using RestTemplate that consumes REST services. And then you will perform unit testing and end-to-end testing for your REST services in your UserRegistrationSystem application using the Spring Test framework.

With RestTemplate, you can make a call to any REST API from a different application. Let's build your REST client using RestTemplate to access the REST API.

Building a REST Client Using RestTemplate

Building a REST client to consume REST services involves building a request and consuming a response containing the JSON data. Spring provides utility classes and templates to ease the consumption of REST services.

RestTemplate

The org.springframework.web.client.RestTemplate in Spring is used to build a REST client to consume REST services. The central class in Spring is RestTemplate, which can be used for synchronous calls by the client to consume RESTful services. RestTemplate is a thread-safe. The RestTemplate is based on Template Method design pattern.

RestTemplate is part of the spring-web.jar file. So, you need to add the spring-web dependency in your Maven pom.xml file when you are building a stand-alone REST client, as shown in Listing 6-1.

Listing 6-1. Maven pom.xml File with spring-web Dependency

```
<dependencies>
        <dependency>
                <groupId>org.springframework.boot</groupId>
                <artifactId>spring-boot-starter-web</artifactId>
        </dependency>
</dependencies>
```

RestTemplate Method

While using RestTemplate, the client has to only provide the URL and parameters (if any) and then extract the result received from the response. RestTemplate takes care of the HTTP connection itself. The RestTemplate class inherits the RestOperations interface specifying a basic set of RESTful operations, and hence RestTemplate provides support for all major HTTP methods, namely, GET, POST, PUT, DELETE, OPTIONS, HEAD, and other HTTP methods to consume RESTful services. Table 6-1 lists the methods provided by RestTemplate for each HTTP method.

Table 6-1. *RestTemplate Methods for HTTP Operations*

HTTP Method	Spring RestTemplate Method
GET	getForObject(java.lang.String, java.lang.Class<T>, java.lang.Object...) getForEntity(java.lang.String, java.lang.Class<T>, java.lang.Object...)
POST	postForLocation(java.lang.String, java.lang.Object, java.lang.Object...) postForObject(java.lang.String, java.lang.Object, java.lang.Class<T>, java.lang.Object...) postForEntity(postForObject(java.lang.String, java.lang.Object, java.lang.Class<T>, java.lang.Object...))
PUT	put(java.lang.String, java.lang.Object, java.lang.Object...)
DELETE	delete(java.lang.String, java.lang.Object...)
HEAD	headForHeaders(java.lang.String, java.lang.Object...)
OPTIONS	optionsForAllow(java.lang.String, java.lang.Object...)
any	exchange(java.lang.String, org.springframework.http.HttpMethod, org.springframework.http.HttpEntity<?>, java.lang.Class<T>, java.lang.Object...)

The method name in RestTemplate indicates the implementation of the respective HTTP method inside the corresponding method and what is going to be returned. For example, the getForEntity method will perform an HTTP GET action on the server and convert the HTTP response into a given type and return this entity to the client. Similarly, the postForObject method will do an HTTP POST action on the server by converting the given object into an HTTP request and returning the response by converting the HTTP response into an object of a given type.

Let's use RestTemplate's methods to consume REST APIs from the UserRegistrationSystem application developed in Chapter 2.

RestTemplate Operation

You will be using RestTemplate to perform operation for HTTP methods. Let's start with a simple GET request example using the getForEntity method to get plain JSON.

HTTP GET Request with Parameter to Retrieve User

You can use either the getForObject or getForEntity method from RestTemplate to make an HTTP GET request. Here, you will be using the getForObject method for the GET request. Spring RestTemplate provides three overloaded versions of the getForObject method, as shown in Table 6-2.

Table 6-2. *Overloaded getForObject Method*

#	Overloaded getForObject Method
| 1 | ```java
@Override
public <T> T getForObject(String url, Class<T> responseType, Object...
uriVariables) throws RestClientException {

        RequestCallback requestCallback =
        acceptHeaderRequestCallback(responseType);
        HttpMessageConverterExtractor<T> responseExtractor =
                new HttpMessageConverterExtractor<T>(responseType,
                getMessageConverters(), logger);
        return execute(url, HttpMethod.GET, requestCallback,
                responseExtractor, uriVariables);
}
``` |
| 2 | ```java
@Override
public <T> T getForObject(String url, Class<T> responseType, Map<String, ?>
uriVariables) throws RestClientException {

RequestCallback requestCallback =
        acceptHeaderRequestCallback(responseType);
        HttpMessageConverterExtractor<T> responseExtractor =
                new HttpMessageConverterExtractor<T>(responseType,
                getMessageConverters(), logger);
        return execute(url, HttpMethod.GET, requestCallback,
                responseExtractor, uriVariables);
}
``` |
| 3 | ```java
@Override
public <T> T getForObject(URI url, Class<T> responseType) throws
RestClientException {

RequestCallback requestCallback =
        acceptHeaderRequestCallback(responseType);
        HttpMessageConverterExtractor<T> responseExtractor =
                new HttpMessageConverterExtractor<T>(responseType,
                getMessageConverters(), logger);
        return execute(url, HttpMethod.GET, requestCallback,
                responseExtractor);
}
``` |

The first two overloaded method contains a URI template as a String, a return value type, and a URI variable, as method arguments. The third overloaded method takes two parameters, namely, the fully formed URI and the returned value type.

Let's create a UserRegistrationClient class inside the package com.apress.ravi.chapter6.client under the src/main/java folder, as shown in Listing 6-2. You will be consuming the getUserById REST API endpoint developed in Chapter 2 for your UserRegistrationSystem application.
```

Listing 6-2. UserRegistrationClient and getForObject Usage

```
package com.apress.ravi.chapter6.client;

import org.springframework.web.client.RestTemplate;
import com.apress.ravi.chapter2.dto.UsersDTO;

public class UserRegistrationClient {

        private static RestTemplate restTemplate = new RestTemplate();
        private static final String USER_REGISTRATION_BASE_URL =
                        "http://localhost:8080/api/user/";

        public UsersDTO getUserById(final Long userId) {
                return restTemplate.getForObject(
                                USER_REGISTRATION_BASE_URL + "/{id}",
                                UsersDTO.class, userId);
        }
}
```

In Listing 6-2, you created a RestTemplate instance at the class level as RestTemplate is thread-safe. You created a class member USER_REGISTRATION_BASE_URL with the value http://localhost:8080/api/user/.

You created a getUserById method to call RestTemplate's getForObject method to consume the REST API from the URL USER_REGISTRATION_BASE_URL + "/{id}". You specified UsersDTO as a second parameter so that RestTemplate will convert the HTTP response content from the server to the UserDTO instance using HttpMessageConverter.

The getUserById method can be tested by creating a main method in the UserRegistrationClient class, as shown in Listing 6-3.

Listing 6-3. Main Method in the UserRegistrationClient Class

```
public static void main(String[] args) {
        UserRegistrationClient userRegistrationClient =
                        new UserRegistrationClient();
        UsersDTO user =
                        userRegistrationClient.getUserById(1L);
        System.out.println("User-ID" + user.getId()
                        + " User-Name" + user.getName());
}
```

Note that before you run the main method, you need to ensure that the UserRegistrationSystem application is up and running.

Getting all users is a little trickier because providing the UsersDTO[] class as a return value type to getForObject would result in an array of the UsersDTO instance, as shown in Listing 6-4.

Listing 6-4. Getting All Users

```
public UsersDTO[] getAllUsers() {
        return restTemplate.getForObject(
                        USER_REGISTRATION_BASE_URL,
                        UsersDTO[].class);
}
```

HTTP POST Request with JSON Data to Create an User

You can use the postForLocation, postForEntity, or postForObject method from RestTemplate to make an HTTP POST request. Here, you will be using the postForObject method for the POST request. Spring RestTemplate provides three overloaded versions of the postForObject method, as shown in Table 6-3.

Table 6-3. *Overloaded postForObject Methods*

#	Overloaded postForObject Method
| 1 | ```
@Override
public <T> T postForObject(String url, Object request,Class<T> responseType,
Object... uriVariables) throws RestClientException {

        RequestCallback requestCallback =
                        httpEntityCallback(request, responseType);
        HttpMessageConverterExtractor<T> responseExtractor =
                        new HttpMessageConverterExtractor<T>(
                                responseType,
                                getMessageConverters(),
                                logger);
        return execute(url, HttpMethod.POST, requestCallback,
                responseExtractor, uriVariables);
}
``` |
| 2 | ```
@Override
public <T> T postForObject(String url, Object request, Class<T>responseType,Map<S
tring,?>uriVariables)throws RestClientException{

        RequestCallback requestCallback =
                        httpEntityCallback(request, responseType);
        HttpMessageConverterExtractor<T> responseExtractor =
                        new HttpMessageConverterExtractor<T>(
                                responseType,
                                getMessageConverters(),
                                logger);
        return execute(url, HttpMethod.POST, requestCallback,
                responseExtractor, uriVariables);
}
``` |
| 3 | ```
@Override
public <T> T postForObject(URI url, Object request,
Class<T> responseType) throws RestClientException {

        RequestCallback requestCallback =
                        httpEntityCallback(request, responseType);
        HttpMessageConverterExtractor<T> responseExtractor =
                        new HttpMessageConverterExtractor<T>(
                                responseType,
                                getMessageConverters());
        return execute(url, HttpMethod.POST, requestCallback,
                responseExtractor);
}
``` |
```

The first two overloaded methods contain the URI template as a String and the request object, return value type, and URI variable as method arguments. The third overloaded method takes three parameters: a fully formed URI, a request object, and a returned value type.

You will use RestTemplate's postForObject method to perform POST operations on the resource http:// localhost:8080/api/user/. The postForObject method from RestTemplate performs the HTTP POST operation of a given URI and object and then converts a response into a representation based on responseType. Listing 6-5 shows the createUser method that creates a new user using POST for the object method.

Listing 6-5. Creating a New User

```
public UsersDTO createUser(final UsersDTO user) {
        return restTemplate.postForObject(
                        USER_REGISTRATION_BASE_URL,
                        user,
                        UsersDTO.class);
}
```

In Listing 6-5, you created a createUser method with an argument of type UsersDTO to call RestTemplate's postForObject method to consume the REST API from the URL USER_REGISTRATION_BASE_URL. You passed the argument's value to the postForObject method as the second parameter. You specified UsersDTO as the third parameter so that RestTemplate will convert the HTTP response content from the server to the UserDTO instance using HttpMessageConverter.

The createUser method can be tested by updating the main method in the UserRegistrationClient class, as shown in Listing 6-6.

Listing 6-6. Main Method in the UserRegistrationClient Class

```
public static void main(String[] args) {
        UserRegistrationClient userRegistrationClient =
                        new UserRegistrationClient();

        UsersDTO user = new UsersDTO();
        user.setName("Soniya Singh");
        user.setAddress("JP Nagar; Bangalore; India");
        user.setEmail("test@test.com");

        UsersDTO newUser = userRegistrationClient.createUser(user);
        System.out.println(newUser.getId());
}
```

HTTP PUT Request with Parameter to Update User

You will be using the put method from RestTemplate to perform an HTTP PUT operation. Spring RestTemplate provides three overloaded version of the put method, as shown in Table 6-4.

Table 6-4. *Overloaded put Method*

#	Overloaded put Method
| 1 | ```java
@Override
public void put(String url, Object request,
        Object... uriVariables) throws RestClientException {
    RequestCallback requestCallback =
                    httpEntityCallback(request);
    execute(url, HttpMethod.PUT, requestCallback,
                    null, uriVariables);
}
``` |
| 2 | ```java
@Override
public void put(String url, Object request,
        Map<String, ?> uriVariables) throws RestClientException {
    RequestCallback requestCallback =
                    httpEntityCallback(request);
    execute(url, HttpMethod.PUT, requestCallback,
                    null, uriVariables);
}
``` |
| 3 | ```java
@Override
public void put(URI url, Object request) throws RestClientException {
    RequestCallback requestCallback =
                    httpEntityCallback(request);
    execute(url, HttpMethod.PUT, requestCallback, null);
}
``` |

The first two overloaded methods contain a URI template as a String and a request object and URI variable as method arguments. The third overloaded method takes two parameters: a fully formed URI and a request object. The put method return type is void. Listing 6-7 shows the updateUser method that will update the UserDTO instance. The put method will not return any response.

Listing 6-7. Update Existing User

```java
public void updateUser(final Long userId, final UsersDTO user) {
    restTemplate.put(
                    USER_REGISTRATION_BASE_URL + "/{id}",
                    user,
                    userId);
}
```

To test updateUser, update the main method with the code shown in Listing 6-8.
```

Listing 6-8. The Updated Main Method

```
public static void main(String[] args) {
        UserRegistrationClient userRegistrationClient =
                        new UserRegistrationClient();

        UsersDTO user = userRegistrationClient.getUserById(1L);
        System.out.println("old user name: " + user.getName());

        user.setName("Ravi Kant Soni");
        userRegistrationClient.updateUser(1L, user);
        System.out.println("updated user name: " + user.getName());
}
```

HTTP DELETE with Parameter to Delete User

There are three overloaded delete methods provided by RestTemplate to support the HTTP DELETE method, as shown in Table 6-5.

Table 6-5. *Overloaded DELETE Method*

#	Overloaded delete Method
1	```@Override public void delete(String url, Object... uriVariables) throws RestClientException { execute(url, HttpMethod.DELETE, null, null, uriVariables); }```
2	```@Override public void delete(String url, Map<String, ?> uriVariables) throws RestClientException { execute(url, HttpMethod.DELETE, null, null, uriVariables); }```
3	```@Override public void delete(URI url) throws RestClientException { execute(url, HttpMethod.DELETE, null, null); }```

The first two overloaded methods contain the URI template as a String and a URI variable as a method argument. The third overloaded method takes only one parameter, that is, a fully formed URI. The delete method return type is void.

Listing 6-9 shows the deleteUser method that will delete the UserDTO instance. The delete method will not return any response.

Listing 6-9. Delete a User

```
public void deleteUser(final Long userId) {
        restTemplate.delete(
                        USER_REGISTRATION_BASE_URL + "/{id}",
                        userId);
}
```

To test this new functionality, update the main method, as shown in Listing 6-10.

Listing 6-10. Updated Main Method

```
public static void main(String[] args) {
        UserRegistrationClient userRegistrationClient =
                        new UserRegistrationClient();

        System.out.println("Old Users List: " +
                        userRegistrationClient.getAllUsers().length);

        userRegistrationClient.deleteUser(1L);

        System.out.println("New Users List: " +
                        userRegistrationClient.getAllUsers().length);
}
```

The RestTemplate Exchange API

Now, let's understand the `RestTemplate` exchange API to perform HTTP operations in a more generic way, as shown in Listing 6-11.

Listing 6-11. Exchange API to Get User

```
public ResponseEntity<UsersDTO> getUserByIdUsingExchangeAPI(final Long userId) {
  HttpEntity<UsersDTO> httpEntity = new HttpEntity<UsersDTO>(new UsersDTO());
        return restTemplate.exchange(USER_REGISTRATION_BASE_URL + "/{id}",
                        HttpMethod.GET, httpEntity, UsersDTO.class,        userId);
}
```

As shown in Listing 6-11, the `RestTemplate`'s exchange method generalizes the return type from the `responseType` parameter passed to this method, and the `ResponseEntity` instance of type `UserDTO` is returned.

To test this functionality, update the main method, as shown in Listing 6-12.

Listing 6-12. Updated Main Method

```
        public static void main(String[] args) {
                UserRegistrationClient userRegistrationClient =
                                new UserRegistrationClient();
```

```
        ResponseEntity<UsersDTO> responseEntity =
                    userRegistrationClient.getUserByIdUsingExchangeAPI(1L);
        UsersDTO user = responseEntity.getBody();
        System.out.println(user.getName());
    }
```

The getBody method of ResponseEntity returns the UsersDTO, as shown in Listing 6-12.

Basic Authentication with RestTemplate

So far you have successfully created a REST client for your UserRegistrationSystem application.

In Chapter 4, you secured your REST APIs, and any communication required Basic Authentication. Without that, the program would raise an HttpClientErrorException with a status code of 401.

To interact with a secure API, you need to programmatically Base64-encode the user's credentials and also construct an authorization request header by prefixing Basic to the encoded value. You will create a class called UserRegistrationClientBasicAuth under the package com.apress.ravi.chapter6.client, as shown in Listing 6-13.

Listing 6-13. UserRegistrationClient with BasicAuth

```
package com.apress.ravi.chapter6.client;

import org.apache.tomcat.util.codec.binary.Base64;
import org.springframework.http.HttpEntity;
import org.springframework.http.HttpHeaders;
import org.springframework.http.HttpMethod;
import org.springframework.web.client.RestTemplate;

public class UserRegistrationClientBasicAuth {

        private static final String securityUserName = "admin";
        private static final String securityUserPassword = "password";

        private static final String USER_REGISTRATION_BASE_URL =
                    "http://localhost:8080/api/user/";

        private static RestTemplate restTemplate = new RestTemplate();

        public void deleteUserById(Long userId) {

                String userCredential =
                            securityUserName + ":" + securityUserPassword;
                byte[] base64UserCredentialData =
                            Base64.encodeBase64(userCredential.getBytes());
```

```
            HttpHeaders authenticationHeaders = new HttpHeaders();
            authenticationHeaders.set("Authorization",
                            "Basic " + new String(base64UserCredentialData));

            HttpEntity<Void> httpEntity =
                            new HttpEntity<Void>(authenticationHeaders);

            restTemplate.exchange(USER_REGISTRATION_BASE_URL + "/{id}",
                            HttpMethod.DELETE, httpEntity, Void.class, userId);
        }
}
```

In Listing 6-13, you have concatenated securityUserName and securityUserPassword, and then Base64 encodes this user credential and creates authenticationHeaders by prefixing Basic to this encoded value. You also created an instance of HttpEntity of type Void by passing authenticationHeaders to its constructor. Finally, you called RestTemplate's exchange method to perform an HTTP DELETE operation with a responseType of Void.

Testing RESTful Services Using the Spring Test Framework

In this section, you will perform unit and end-to-end testing of the RESTful services developed in Chapter 2. You will focus on two flavors of testing: unit testing and integration testing. Unit testing is used to verify an isolated unit of code. Integration testing is used to focus on interaction between previously tested code/units.

What Is Testing?

Testing is a crucial part of the software development life cycle; it is the process that ensures the quality and performance of the software, without which the software development could be completed.

Unit testing means testing each component of an application independently or separately, whereas *integration testing* helps in ensuring that multiple components in a system are working well.

It is a good practice to create unit test in a separate source folder such as src/test/java or in a separate project. What should be tested is a hot topic where some developers believe that every statement in the code should be tested.

You can do testing either automatically or manually. The benefits of automated testing are that it runs continuously and repeatedly at different phases of software development process, which is highly recommended when you follow the agile development process. Since the Spring Framework is agile in nature, it supports this kind of process.

Let's discuss a popular Java testing framework, JUnit, and the basic techniques of testing with it.

Testing Using JUnit4

JUnit4 (http://junit.org/) is a popular unit testing framework on the Java platform. It provides the @Test annotation to annotate a method that needs to be tested. A test method inside the Test class needs to be annotated with the @org.junit.Test annotation. JUnit frameworks provide different annotations and assert methods to perform unit testing.

JUnit 4 Annotations

Table 6-6 lists the annotations provided by the JUnit framework.

Table 6-6. *Annotations in the JUnit Framework*

Annotation	Import	Description
@Test	org.junit.Test	Annotates the public void method with the @Test annotation to identify and run test cases.
@Before	org.junit.Before	Annotates the public void method with the @Before annotation, which needs to be executed before each test method in that class. This method can be used to set up environment variables.
@After	org.junit.After	Annotates the public void method with the @After annotation, which needs to be executed after each test method in that class. This method can be used to clean up the test environment or to release resources.
@BeforeClass	org.junit.BeforeClass	Annotates the public static void method with the @BeforeClass annotation, which needs to be executed only once before the entire test executes in that Test class.
@AfterClass	org.junit.AfterClass	Annotates the public static void method with the @AfterClass annotation, which needs to be executed only once after the entire test executes in that Test class. This method can be used to perform some cleanup activities.
@Ignore	org.junit.Ignore	Annotates the method with the @Ignore annotation, which shouldn't be executed.

JUnit 4 Assert Methods

The JUnit framework provides the org.junit.Assert class, which contains a set of assert methods useful for writing unit tests to test certain conditions. These methods compare the expected value with the actual value to verify the test result. Table 6-7 lists a few of the assert methods provided by JUnit 4.

Table 6-7. *Annotations in the JUnit Framework*

Assert Method	Description
assertTrue(boolean expected, boolean actual)	This method checks whether the Boolean condition is true.
assertFalse(boolean condition)	The assertFalse method checks whether the Boolean condition is false.
assertEquals(boolean expected, expected, actual)	The assertEquals compares the equality of any two objects using the equals() method.
assertEquals(boolean expected, expected, actual, tolerance)	The assertEquals method compares either the float or the double values, and tolerance defines the number of the decimal that must be the same.
assertNull(Object object)	The assertNotNull tests that a given object is null.
assertNotNull(Object object)	The assertNotNull tests that a given object is not null.
assertSame(Object object1,Object object2)	The assertSame method tests whether two objects refer to the same object.
assertNotSame(Object object1,Object object2)	The assertNotSame method tests whether two objects do not refer to the same object.

Example: Implementing JUnit 4

Let's develop a simple application to add two numbers, as shown in Listing 6-14.

Listing 6-14. Simple Calculator to Perform an Add Operation

```
package com.apress.ravi.chapter6.SpringTesting;

public class SimpleCalculator {

        public long addOperation(int x, int y) {
                return x + y;
        }
}
```

Note that the JUnit4 JAR needs to be added in the application's CLASSPATH to compile and run the test cases created for JUnit 4.

Now, you will be testing your simple addOperation method in the SimpleCalculator class with JUnit 4. The STS IDE supports the creation of JUnit tests through wizards. You will create your test class SimpleCalculatorTests, as shown in Listing 6-15.

Listing 6-15. Test Add Operation Method

```java
package com.apress.ravi.chapter6.SpringTesting;

import static org.junit.Assert.assertEquals;

import org.junit.After;
import org.junit.Before;
import org.junit.Test;

public class SimpleCalculatorTests {

        private SimpleCalculator simpleCalculator;

        @Before
        public void setup() {
                simpleCalculator = new SimpleCalculator();
        }

        @Test
        public void verifyAdd() {
                long sum = simpleCalculator.addOperation(2, 1);
                assertEquals(3, sum);
        }

        @After
        public void teardown() {
                simpleCalculator = null;
        }
}
```

In Listing 6-15, the setup method is annotated with the @Before annotation to perform the initialization of an instance member variable, and it instructs JUnit to run this setup method prior to any test method execution in the SimpleCalculatorTests class. The teardown method is annotated with the @After annotation and instructs JUnit to run the teardown method to perform cleanup after any test method execution in the SimpleCalculatorTests class.

The verifyAdd method is annotated with the @Test annotation to denote verifyAdd as a JUnit test method. The verifyAdd method contains code that ensures that your production code works as expected.

Now, run your test case by right-clicking the test class and choosing RUN AS JUnit test. The JUnit view helps verify the success or failure of your test. On successfully passing the JUnit test, the result view will display a green bar, as shown in Figure 6-1.

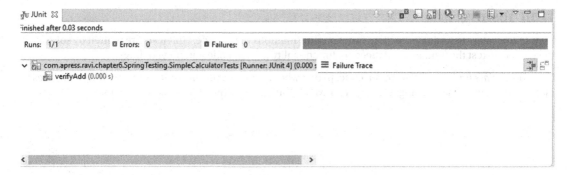

Figure 6-1. *A green bar shows a test passing successfully*

On the failure of the JUnit test, the result view will display a red bar, as shown in Figure 6-2.

```
@Test
public void verifyAdd() {
        long sum = simpleCalculator.addOperation(2, 1);
        assertEquals(2, sum);
}
```

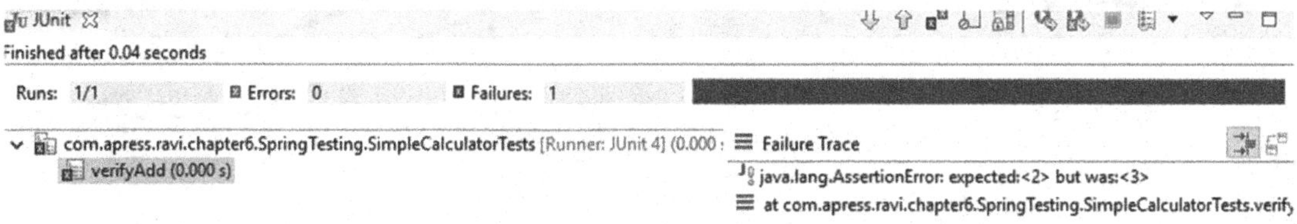

Figure 6-2. *A red bar shows that a test failed*

Agile Software Testing

In the software development world, *agile* refers to a project management approach where teams work by focusing on the principles of collaboration, flexibility, simplicity, and responsiveness throughout the development of new modules in an application. When using the agile software methodology, a team delivers the project or allocated works in smaller divisions termed *sprints* with continuous collaboration between a cross-functional team including stakeholders. This particular methodology is incremental and iterative in nature, focusing on the effective delivery of allocated works.

Agile software testing refers to the practice of testing software for any bugs and performance issues within the context of the agile workflow. It includes unit testing as well as integration testing. The following sections will help you understand the objectives of unit testing and integration testing.

Unit Testing

Unit testing refers to testing individual functionality/methods in the code. Unit tests are written by software developers to test the fundamental pieces of functionality in their code and prevent bugs.

The phrase *class under test* refers to the concept that whenever you write any unit test cases, you create a test class against a class that is being tested and for which you have to write unit test cases, as shown in Figure 6-3.

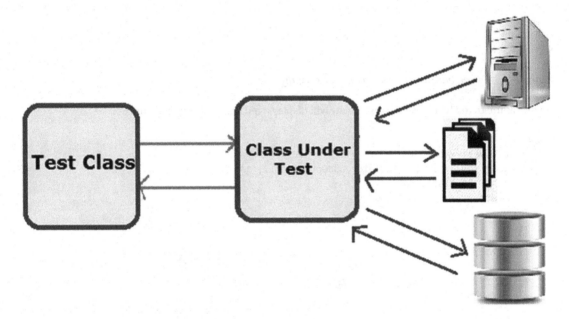

Figure 6-3. *Class under test and its dependencies*

Let's take an example where you have two classes named UserRegistrationService and UserRegistrationDAO to perform a CRUD operation by interacting with a database. The UserRegistrationService class needs the UserRegistrationDAO object for loading a list of users from a database. This UserRegistrationDAO object is a real object, so while testing your UserRegistrationService class, you need to have a UserRegistrationDAO object with a valid connection to the database. You also have to insert a user in the database for the testing. Setting up a database connection, inserting a user into the database, and then testing the UserRegistrationService class can be a lot of work.

Unit Testing for the Dependent Class with a Mocking Object

You can reduce this work effort by creating a fake UserRegistrationDAO instance that will return an expected user list and pass it to UserRegistrationService. This fake UserRegistrationDAO will not have a connection to a database. This fake UserRegistrationDAO object is called a *mock* object and is a replacement for the realUserRegistrationDAO object. This will ease the testing of the UserRegistrationService class. Figure 6-4 shows how to mock a dependency for a class under test.

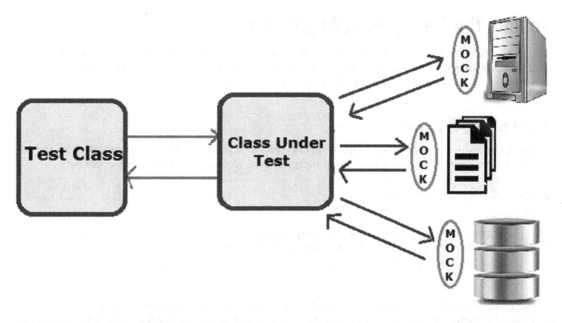

Figure 6-4. *Mock dependent object in class under test*

The Mockito Framework

The Mockito framework is an open source Mock framework for creating and configuring mock objects.

Again, a *mock* object is a fake object that mimics an actual object, and the process of creating fake object is called *mocking*. Several libraries are available in Java that can be used for mocking, such as EasyMock and Mockito.

To use Mockito, you need to have a Mockito JAR along with JUnit in an application context. Mockito supports field-level annotation as listed here:

- @Mock: This annotation is used to create a mock object for an annotated field.

- @Spy: This annotation creates a *spy* for the real object field it annotates, which can be referred to as a *partial mock*, when spying or stubbing a specific method of it.

- @RunWith(MockitoJUnitRunner.class): Creating a mock object using the @Mock annotation and the @Spy annotation requires the @RunWith(MockitoJUnitRunner. class) annotation to be applied to your test class. When MockitoJUnitRunner executes the unit test, all annotated fields will create mock and spy objects.

Refer to http://mockito.org/ to get more details about the Mockito framework.

Integration Testing

In integration testing, individual modules are combined and logically tested as a group. Integration testing in the software development phase occurs after unit testing.

Testing the Spring Boot Application

The spring-test module in the Spring Framework allows developers to perform unit testing and integration testing by providing rich sets of annotations, utility classes, and mock objects. Let's set up the environment by updating your Maven pom.xml file with the required dependency.

Maven Dependency

Spring Boot provides the starter POM named spring-boot-starter-test, which automatically adds the spring-test module to the Spring Boot application. Listing 6-16 shows the dependency in pom.xml.

Listing 6-16. Dependency in pom.xml

```
<dependency>
        <groupId>org.springframework.boot</groupId>
        <artifactId>spring-boot-starter-test</artifactId>
        <scope>test</scope>
</dependency>
```

This starter POM brings JUnit (the de facto standard for unit testing a Java application), AssertJ (an assertion library), Mockito (a Java mocking framework), and Spring Test and Spring Boot Test (utilities and integration test support for Spring Boot applications) to your application, as shown in Figure 6-5.

Figure 6-5. JAR in classpath

Annotations in Spring Testing

The Spring Framework provides different annotations that developers can use to perform unit and integration testing.

Let's examine typical test cases to understand the spring-test module and annotations provided by the Spring Framework. Listing 6-17 shows an example of Spring Test built using Spring Boot Test.

Listing 6-17. Unit Testing Using Spring Boot Test

```
package com.apress.ravi.chapter6.UserRegistrationSystem;

import org.junit.After;
import org.junit.Before;
import org.junit.Test;
import org.junit.runner.RunWith;
import org.springframework.boot.test.context.SpringBootTest;
import org.springframework.test.context.junit4.SpringRunner;

@RunWith(SpringRunner.class)
@SpringBootTest(classes = UserRegistrationSystemApplication.class,
                webEnvironment = WebEnvironment.RANDOM_PORT)
public class UserRegistrationSystemApplicationTests {

        @Before
        public void setup() {
        }

        @Test
        public void testFunction() {
        }

        @After
        public void teardown() {
        }
}
```

Listing 6-17 contains three methods: setup, testFunction, and teardown. Each method is annotated with the JUnit annotation.

- @RunWith(SpringRunner.class): The @RunWith(SpringRunner.class)annotation instructs JUnit to use the SpringJUnit4ClassRunner class to run the test case. The SpringRunner class extends the SpringJUnit4ClassRunner class. The @RunWith annotation is a JUnit annotation; it executes the tests in a class annotated with the @RunWith annotation or extends another class annotated with the @RunWith annotation. This means the annotated test class will not be executed by the built-in API in the JUnit framework. Rather, it will use SpringJUnit4ClassRunner for running the test cases within the SpringApplicationContext environment.

- @SpringBootTest: Spring Boot provides the @SpringBootTest annotation to bootstrap with Spring Boot's support; it is an alternative to the standard Spring Test @ContextConfiguration annotation when you need to have Spring Boot features. The @ContextConfiguration annotation is used to test the application context for the test class. It caches ApplicationContext and puts it in static memory for the entire duration of the test or test suite, and the entire test executes in the same JVM because ApplicationContext is stored in the static memory.

- webEnvironment: The webEnvironment attribute of @SpringBootTest configures the web environment for the test. It lets the developer test with a mock servlet environment or with a real HTTP server running on either a DEFINED_PORT or RANDOM_PORT.

- classes: You can use the classes attribute of @SpringBootTest to load a specific configuration. By default, it will search for the @SpringBootApplication class to load @Configuration.

Unit Testing REST Controller

Inversion of Control (IoC) in the Spring Framework makes unit testing easier by supplying dependency injection. Dependency can be easily mocked with expected behaviors by allowing developers to test code in isolation.

The traditional approach to test Spring MVC controllers follows this concept. Listing 6-18 shows the unit testing for the listAllUsers method in the UserRegistrationRestController class.

Listing 6-18. Unit Testing for REST Controller

```
package com.apress.ravi.chapter6.UserRegistrationSystem;

import java.util.ArrayList;
import java.util.List;

import static org.mockito.Mockito.when;

import org.junit.After;
import org.junit.Assert;
import org.junit.Before;
import org.junit.Test;
import org.junit.runner.RunWith;
import org.mockito.Mock;
import org.mockito.Spy;
import org.springframework.boot.test.context.SpringBootTest;
import org.springframework.boot.test.context.SpringBootTest.WebEnvironment;
import org.springframework.http.HttpStatus;
import org.springframework.http.ResponseEntity;
import org.springframework.test.context.junit4.SpringRunner;
import org.springframework.test.util.ReflectionTestUtils;

import com.apress.ravi.chapter2.UserRegistrationSystemApplication;
import com.apress.ravi.chapter2.Rest.UserRegistrationRestController;
import com.apress.ravi.chapter2.dto.UsersDTO;
import com.apress.ravi.chapter2.repository.UserJpaRepository;

@RunWith(SpringRunner.class)
@SpringBootTest(classes = UserRegistrationSystemApplication.class,
        webEnvironment = WebEnvironment.RANDOM_PORT)
public class UserRegistrationRestControllerTest{
```

```java
@Spy
private UserRegistrationRestController userRegistrationRestController;

@Mock
private UserJpaRepository userJpaRepository;

@Before
public void setup() {
userRegistrationRestController = new UserRegistrationRestController();
ReflectionTestUtils.setField(userRegistrationRestController,
                    "userJpaRepository", userJpaRepository);
}

@Test
public void testListAllUsers() {

List<UsersDTO> userList = new ArrayList<UsersDTO>();
userList.add(new UsersDTO());
when(this.userJpaRepository.findAll()).thenReturn(userList);

ResponseEntity<List<UsersDTO>> responseEntity =
                    this.userRegistrationRestController.listAllUsers();

Assert.assertEquals(HttpStatus.OK, responseEntity.getStatusCode());
Assert.assertEquals(1, responseEntity.getBody().size());
}

@After
public void teardown() {
userRegistrationRestController = null;
}
}
```

In Listing 6-18, you have created a UserRegistrationRestControllerTest test class under the package com. apress.ravi.chapter6.UserRegistrationSystem inside the folder src/test/java. You have annotated this class with the @RunWith(SpringRunner.class) annotation that supports the mocking of dependent Object and @SpringBootTest(classes = UserRegistrationSystemApplication.class, webEnvironment = WebEnvironment.RANDOM_PORT) annotation. The webEnvironment=RANDOM_PORT part starts the server with a random port (useful to avoid conflicts in test environments).

The UserRegistrationRestControllerTest class uses Mockito's @Spy annotation to spy UserRegistrationRestController. This test class uses the @Mock annotation to mock UserRegistrationRestController's only dependency: UserJpaRepository.

In the setup method, you create an instance of UserRegistrationRestController and inject the mock UserJpaRepository using Spring's ReflectionTestUtils utility class by calling its setField method. You annotated the setup class with the @Before annotation.

In the testListAllUsers method, you used Mockito's when and then return methods to set the UserJpaRepository mock's behavior. You also indicated that when the UserJpaRepository's findAll method is invoked, a list of users should be returned. Finally, you invoked the listAllUsers method and the assert controller's return value.

In the teardown method, you assigned a null value to UserRegistrationRestController and annotated this method with the @After annotation.

When you run the test class as a JUnit test, you can view the result in JUnit view, as shown in Figure 6-6.

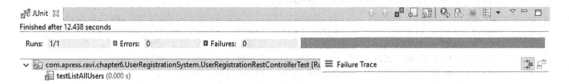

Figure 6-6. *JUnit view*

As shown in Figure 6-6, UserRegistrationRestControllerTest has been treated as a POJO and hence doesn't test the controller's request mapping validation. So, in the next section, you will be using the Spring MVC Test framework that allows you to test a controller as MVC's controller. So, DispatcherServlet will intercept the request and generate a response the same as when it runs in a web container when actually starting up a web server.

Testing the Web Layer Using the Spring MVC Test Framework

In this section, you will do testing with the @WebMvcTest annotation, which can be used in combination with @RunWith(SpringRunner.class) for a typical Spring MVC test and which can be used when a test focuses only on Spring MVC components. A test class annotated with @WebMvcTest will autoconfigure MockMvc(include support for HtmlUnit WebClient and Selenium WebDriver).

Generally, @WebMvcTest is used in combination with @MockBean to create any collaborators required by your @Controller beans. To start with the Spring MVC Test framework, you need to be familiar with MockMVC.

MockMvc

The MockMvc class is the central class of the Spring MVC Test framework. The org.springframework.test.web.servlet.MockMvc class can be used to write the test for the applications developed using the Spring MVC framework. The MockMvc class can be used to perform HTTP requests.

MockMvc mock the entire Spring infrastructure and is created using the implementation of the org.springframework.test.web.servlet.MockMvcBuilder interface, which makes the Spring MVC Test framework heavily use the Builder pattern.

The MockMvc class contains the perform method, which can be used to run test cases by passing a relative path. After that, the Expect method can be used to verify the different components inside the controller.

The andExpect (status().OK()) line can be used to verify the 200 status. Similarly, contentType validation, XPath validation, data validation model, URL validation, and so on, can be performed.

Let's create the UserRegistrationControllerTest class in the package com.apress.ravi.chapter6.UserRegistrationSystem under the src/test/java folder, as shown in Listing 6-19, to demonstrate how to test the UserRegistrationRestController's getUserById method. You will also mock the dependencies that the controller requires.

Listing 6-19. Testing the Web Layer Using Spring MVC Test

```java
package com.apress.ravi.chapter6.UserRegistrationSystem;

import static org.hamcrest.Matchers.is;
import static org.mockito.Mockito.when;
import static org.springframework.test.web.servlet.request.MockMvcRequestBuilders.get;
import static org.springframework.test.web.servlet.result.MockMvcResultHandlers.print;
import static org.springframework.test.web.servlet.result.MockMvcResultMatchers.content;
import static org.springframework.test.web.servlet.result.MockMvcResultMatchers.jsonPath;
import static org.springframework.test.web.servlet.result.MockMvcResultMatchers.status;

import java.nio.charset.Charset;

import org.junit.Before;
import org.junit.Test;
import org.junit.runner.RunWith;
import org.springframework.beans.factory.annotation.Autowired;
import org.springframework.boot.test.autoconfigure.web.servlet.WebMvcTest;
import org.springframework.boot.test.mock.mockito.MockBean;
import org.springframework.http.MediaType;
import org.springframework.test.context.ContextConfiguration;
import org.springframework.test.context.junit4.SpringRunner;
import org.springframework.test.web.servlet.MockMvc;

import com.apress.ravi.chapter2.UserRegistrationSystemApplication;
import com.apress.ravi.chapter2.Rest.UserRegistrationRestController;
import com.apress.ravi.chapter2.dto.UsersDTO;
import com.apress.ravi.chapter2.repository.UserJpaRepository;;

@RunWith(SpringRunner.class)
@WebMvcTest(controllers = UserRegistrationRestController.class)
@ContextConfiguration(classes = UserRegistrationSystemApplication.class)
public class UserRegistrationControllerTest {

        @Autowired
        private MockMvc mockMvc;

        @MockBean
        private UserJpaRepository userJpaRepositoryMock;

        private MediaType contentType;
        private UsersDTO user;

        @Before
        public void setup() {
                contentType = new MediaType(MediaType.APPLICATION_JSON.getType(),
                                MediaType.APPLICATION_JSON.getSubtype(),
                                Charset.forName("utf8"));
```

```
                user = new UsersDTO();
                user.setName("Ravi Kant Soni");
                user.setAddress("JP Nagar; Bangalore; India");
                user.setEmail("ravikantsoni.author@gmail.com");
        }

        @Test
        public void shouldReturnSuccessMessage() throws Exception {

                when(this.userJpaRepositoryMock.findById(1L)).thenReturn(user);

                this.mockMvc.perform(get("/api/user/1"))
                .andExpect(status().isOk())
                .andExpect(content().contentType(contentType))
                .andExpect(jsonPath("$.name", is("Ravi Kant Soni")))
                .andExpect(jsonPath("$.address",
                        is("JP Nagar; Bangalore; India")))
                .andExpect(jsonPath("$.email",
                        is("ravikantsoni.author@gmail.com")))
                .andDo(print());
        }
}
```

Let's look at Listing 6-19 in detail. In it, you tested the behavior of UserRegistrationRestController's getUserById method.

- *@RunWith, @WebMvcTest, and @ContextConfiguration*: You have used the @ContextConfiguration annotation to look for the main configuration class. The @WebMvcTest annotation is used to test the web layer. So, Spring Boot will instantiate the web layer, not the whole context.

- *@Autowired MockMvc*: You have autowired MockMvc instead of building it manually. So, Spring will create and configure MockMvc and inject it at runtime. An @Autowired MockMvc combined with @WebMvcTest(controllers=UserRegistrationRestControl le.class) gives a fully configured MockMvc instance.

  Using MockMvc, you sent mock HTTP requests to UserRegistrationRestController and tested how UserRegistrationRestController behaves without running this controller within a server.

- *@MockBean*: You annotated UserJpaRepository with the @MockBean annotation to create and inject a mock of UserJpaRepository.

- *@Before*: You annotated the setup method with the @Before annotation. You created and initialized the MediaType (contentType) and UserDTO (user) domain objects that have been used in the @Test method.

- *@Test*: You annotated the shouldReturnSuccessMessage method with the @Test annotation. You have used Mockito to stub the findById method on the UserJpaRepository mock to return the initialized UserDTO instance.

  You used the MockMvcRequestBuilders class's get to create a GET request. MockMvcRequestBuilders also provides additional methods such as post, put, and delete to create corresponding HTTP requests.

You have called MockMvc's perform to make a GET request to "/api/user/{id}" and the Expect method to perform assert the response:

- HTTP status code 200 in response.

- The contentType in the response content.

- The properties (name, address, e-mail) of the user attribute against the values you used to initialize UserDTO. You have used the JsonPath expression in the jsonPath method to write assertions against the response body. Put simply, JsonPath for JSON is the same as xPath for XML.

Finally, you have used andDo(print()) to get the following output on the console:

```
MockHttpServletRequest:
      HTTP Method = GET
      Request URI = /api/user/1
       Parameters = {}
          Headers = {}

Handler:
             Type = com.apress.ravi.chapter2.Rest.UserRegistrationRestController
           Method = public org.springframework.http.ResponseEntity<com.apress.ra
vi.chapter2.dto.UsersDTO> com.apress.ravi.chapter2.Rest.UserRegistrationRestCont
roller.getUserById(java.lang.Long)

Async:
    Async started = false
     Async result = null

Resolved Exception:
             Type = null

ModelAndView:
        View name = null
             View = null
            Model = null

FlashMap:
       Attributes = null

MockHttpServletResponse:
           Status = 200
    Error message = null
          Headers = {Content-Type=[application/json;charset=UTF-8]}
     Content type = application/json;charset=UTF-8
             Body = {"id":null,"name":"Ravi Kant Soni","address":"JP Nagar; Bang
alore; India","email":"ravikantsoni.author@gmail.com"}
    Forwarded URL = null
   Redirected URL = null
          Cookies = []
```

When you run the test, the JUnit view of the test result looks like Figure 6-7.

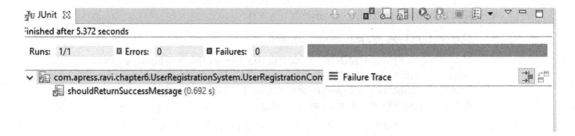

Figure 6-7. JUnit view of test

Summary

In this chapter, you created a REST client using RestTemplate and used it to perform client operations such as GET, POST, PUT, and DELETE on resources. You looked into the different RestTemplate methods and operations to consume REST APIs. You also implemented Basic Authentication with RestTemplate.

Then you moved into testing RESTful services using the Spring Test framework. I introduced unit testing and integration testing. You saw different annotations and assert methods in the JUnit4 framework. Then you looked at a mocking framework and mock objects. Finally, you tested REST services using the Test framework and the Spring MVC Test framework.

In the next chapter, you will manage and monitor your Spring Boot application in production.

CHAPTER 7

■ ■ ■

Application Monitoring Using Spring Boot Actuator

Application monitoring ensures that an application running on a server performs as expected. In Chapter 2, you developed RESTful services using Spring Boot. In addition, Spring Boot supports additional features to monitor and manage your Spring Boot application when it is pushed to production.

For example, say a developer just finished his application and pushed the changes to the repository. Moving on, the developer approaches the operations (ops) team and asks them to deploy this application. In return, the ops team asks the developer for the runbook (i.e., the operational guide), which contains instruction for the deployment, the actions that need to be performed when an exception occurs, and so on. The ops team also needs details on the configuration of applications. A seasoned developer will even share information about external properties and their locations on the server, which the ops team will use to configure external properties with acceptable values. So far so good.

The final question from the ops team is, "How do you monitor this application?" Uh-oh, this was not mentioned in business requirement. So, the developer thinks about the different options, such as asking his manager for more money to develop a monitoring tool, which may not be possible.

The Spring Framework is one of the most popular frameworks for building complex enterprise applications. These applications used to be run on many servers for many domains and environments such as a local build environment, a test environment, a QA environment, and sometimes a user acceptance testing (UAT) environment, before being deployed into the production environment. Each environment had different configurations, such as in the local environment the developer might be using an open source database, and in the production environment the database might be Oracle. Furthermore, the local environment might be using ActiveMQ for messaging, and production might be using an IBM messaging source. There are lots of things that need to be addressed for enterprise needs such as continuous builds, and so on. It's not like you can just create a `.war` file and put it on the server. In this chapter, you will be using a local environment for deployment.

Using HTTP endpoints, you can manage your deployed application in a production environment. Spring Boot has a bunch of features that let you monitor your Spring Boot application in production, or any environment, after you have deployed your application.

In Spring Boot, you can monitor and manage your Spring Boot application in various ways such as HTTP, JVM, and SSH. In this chapter, you will look in the Actuator module from Spring Boot to monitor your application. This chapter will give you an overview of how DevOps uses Spring Boot. DevOps is a combination of dev (a developer) and ops (the operations team).

© Ravi Kant Soni 2017

R. K. Soni, *Full Stack AngularJS for Java Developers*, https://doi.org/10.1007/978-1-4842-3198-2_7

Introducing Spring Boot Actuator

Spring Boot Actuator is a subproject of Spring Boot. The Actuator module in Spring Boot enables production-ready features to be used in your Spring Boot application. Actuator exposes various endpoints to monitor metrics and statistics of your running application. Using Actuator, you can monitor health, view metrics, collect logs, perform thread dumps, understand garbage collection, view environment variables, and view beans from BeanFactory. In addition, you can use it monitor your application for any production support and related stuff such as monitoring processes, checking health, checking whether a process is running, checking whether the database connection is running, and checking related metrics such as heap size or available space in the JVM. All this stuff is taken care of by Actuator.

Spring Boot offers libraries that can expose some REST endpoints so that different monitoring tools can use those REST endpoints to get the data out of the REST endpoints. You can access all these endpoints using <host>:port/<endpoint>. For example, if you want to monitor the health of your application, you have to visit http://localhost:8080/health.

Enabling the Actuator Module

To enable the Actuator module, visit http://start.spring.io/ in your browser. The Ops section on the Spring Initializr site contains a bunch of dependencies, such as Actuator, Actuator Docs, and Remote Shell, as shown in Figure 7-1.

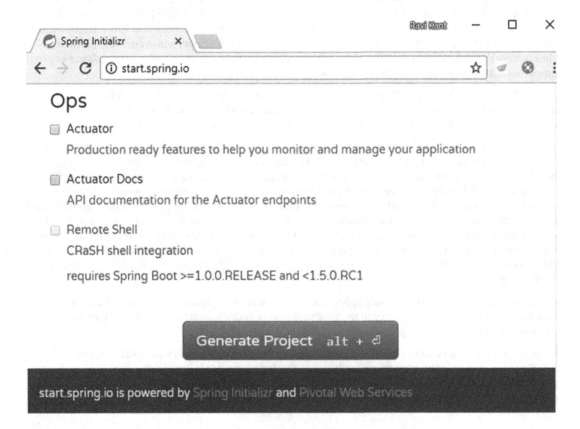

Figure 7-1. Spring Boot starter dependencies in Spring Initializr

Let's manually add the spring-boot-starter-actuator dependency in your Maven pom.xml file in your UserRegistrationSystem application, as shown in Listing 7-1.

Listing 7-1. Actuator Dependency

```
<dependency>
        <groupId>org.springframework.boot</groupId>
        <artifactId>spring-boot-starter-actuator</artifactId>
</dependency>
```

Just by adding the spring-boot-starter-actuator dependency in your pom.xml file, the Actuator module will be enabled in your Spring Boot application and health, metrics, and other features can be automatically applied to your application.

Actuator Endpoints

The Actuator endpoint allows developers to monitor the running Spring Boot application, and it also lets developers interact with the Spring Boot application. Spring Boot provides many built-in endpoints such as a health endpoint that provides basic health information about your running Spring Boot application and that will be mapped to /health. You can also add your own endpoints.

By default, Spring Boot Actuator is secured so that not just anyone can access these endpoints. You can disable these security features by setting properties in the application.properties file, as shown here:

management.security.enabled=false

However, since these actuator endpoints are exposing environment variables and metrics information, you'll want to keep them secured.

Let's start the UserRegistrationSystem application and explore the most common endpoints that Spring Boot provides out of the box. Figure 7-2 shows the endpoints in the STS console.

Figure 7-2. *Endpoints in console*

As shown in Figure 7-2, there are different endpoints that come in the STS console. By default, you have /info, /health, /beans, /dump, /env, and more. All these endpoints are REST endpoints provided by Actuator. Let's explore a few of these REST endpoints so you can fetch data in the next sections.

/info

This endpoint displays arbitrary information about the Spring Boot application. Figure 7-3 shows the /info endpoint in the browser.

Figure 7-3. *The /info endpoint in the browser displays nothing*

As shown in Figure 7-3, by default the /info endpoint displays nothing. You can override this information, though. Still, the /info endpoint displays nonsensitive data.

/env

The /env endpoint returns all the sensitive information that you have configured inside the JVM such as {"local.server.port":8080}. In other words, it displays the port on which your application is running, and it displays system properties such as the JDK and Java versions (jre1.8.0_101\\bin), directory information (user.dir) where your project is running, the library path (java.library.path), the time zone (user.timezone":"Asia/Calcutta"), and so on. It also shows properties information and the properties file name where you have added properties, such as [classpath:/application.properties]":{"management.security.enabled":"false"}. Figure 7-4 shows a cropped image of the /env data in the browser.

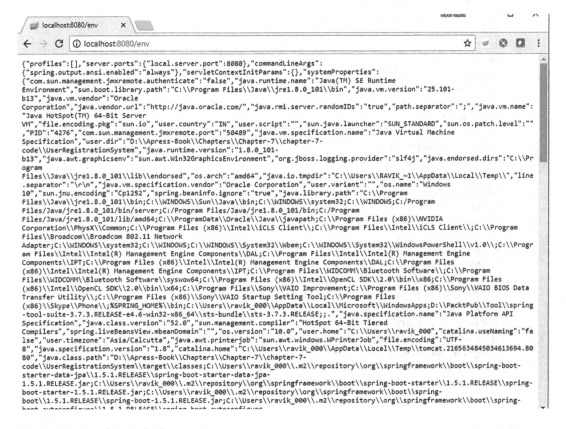

Figure 7-4. */env data in the browser*

/metrics

This endpoint displays information from the OS, the JVM, and application-level metrics such as the memory heap, processor, threads, classloader, and thread pools.

It shows the metrics information for the currently running application. It is sensitive by default. The metric information returns the following data, as shown in Figure 7-5:

```
{
        "mem":295288,
        "mem.free":177815,
        "processors":4,
        "instance.uptime":620849,
        "uptime":632125,
        "systemload.average":-1.0,
        "heap.committed":225792,
        "heap.init":65536,
        "heap.used":47976,
        "heap":905216,
        "nonheap.committed":71360,
        "nonheap.init":2496,
        "nonheap.used":69497,
        "nonheap":0,
        "threads.peak":20,
        "threads.daemon":18,
        "threads.totalStarted":26,
        "threads":20,
        "classes":9559,
        "classes.loaded":9559,
        "classes.unloaded":0,
        "gc.ps_scavenge.count":12,
        "gc.ps_scavenge.time":169,
        "gc.ps_marksweep.count":2,
        "gc.ps_marksweep.time":219,
        "httpsessions.max":-1,"httpsessions.active":0,
        "datasource.primary.active":0,
        "datasource.primary.usage":0.0,
        "gauge.response.userregistrationsystemhealth":214.0,
        "gauge.response.info":37.0,
        "counter.status.200.info":1,
        "counter.status.200.userregistrationsystemhealth":1
}
```

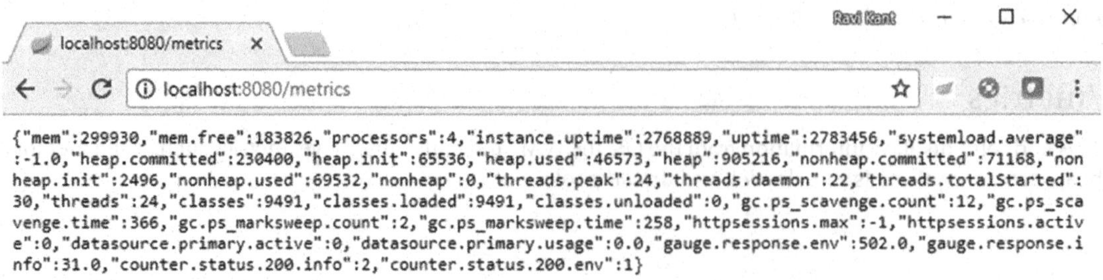

Figure 7-5. /metrics endpoint

As shown in Figure 7-5, you can see metrics information using the /metrics endpoint. This endpoint shows the heap.used details, nonheap.used details, how much memory is free (mem.free), the number of processors being used, instance uptime information, the number of threads, and so on.

/trace

This endpoint displays the trace information requests that have been made by showing a list of REST endpoints people have been accessing. For example, in Figure 7-6, you can see that I have accessed / metrics, /env, and /info. This shows the last few requests that were hit for these particular endpoints. The /trace endpoint also shows the different REST endpoints people have been accessing. If you go to / trace, you can see the last request people have been accessing by the particular REST service.

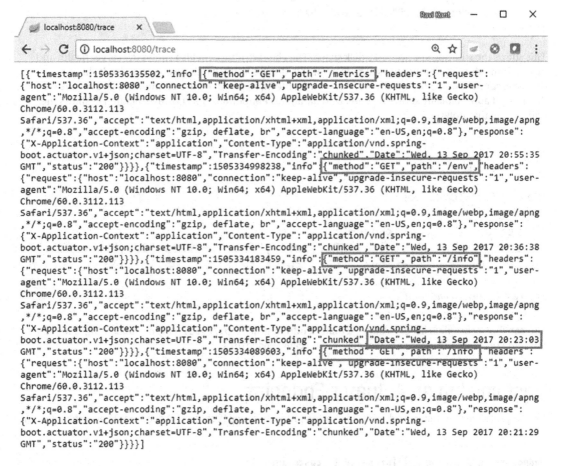

Figure 7-6. /trace endpoint

/health

This endpoint can be used to check the health or status of the running Spring Boot application. It helps developers to monitor the software's health and trace status if the production environment goes down. The default information shown when accessing over HTTP is as follows:

```
{
        "status":"UP",
        "diskSpace":{"status":"UP",
                        "total":142753132544,
                        "free":97978245120,
                        "threshold":10485760
                },
        "db":{"status":"UP","database":"H2","hello":1}
}
```

This shows the running application's disk space. The /health endpoint also shows the server health and gives information on whether the server is up or not. If there is any database connectivity, it shows the database connection automatically. So, if you have autowired any database connection, let's say the H2 database, it automatically shows up here. By default, this endpoint is not sensitive. Figure 7-7 shows the endpoint in the browser.

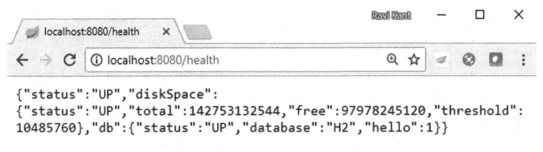

Figure 7-7. /health endpoint

You can find a complete list of existing Actuator endpoints at http://docs.spring.io/spring-boot/docs/current/reference/htmlsingle/#production-ready-endpoints.

Customizing an Actuator Endpoint

You can customize Actuator endpoints via Spring properties (application.properties) using the following format:

endpoints.[endpoint-name].[property to customize]

Properties to Customize

Three properties are available to customize Actuator endpoints.

- id: This is the property by which the endpoint will be accessed over HTTP.

- enabled: This endpoint gives access control to the endpoint. If it is set as true, then this endpoint can be accessed; otherwise, it cannot be.

- sensitive: This property provides a security layer to the endpoint. If it is set as true, then the required authorization shows critical information over HTTP.

For example, you can customize the id, sensitive, and enabled properties of the /health endpoint by adding the following properties in the application.properties file:

```
endpoints.health.id=userregistrationsystemhealth
endpoints.health.enabled=true
endpoints.health.sensitive=false
```

Once you start your application, /userregistrationsystemhealth will appear in the console, as shown in Figure 7-8.

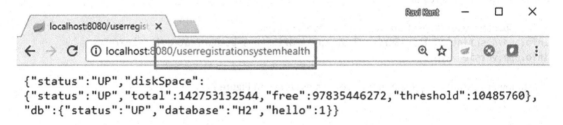

```
{"status":"UP","diskSpace":
{"status":"UP","total":142753132544,"free":97835446272,"threshold":10485760},
"db":{"status":"UP","database":"H2","hello":1}}
```

Figure 7-8. */userregistrationsystemhealth endpoint in the console*

The prefix endpoints is used to identify the endpoint that is being configured in your application. You can access this customized /health endpoint using /userregistrationsystemhealth, as shown in Figure 7-9.

```
{"app":{"description":"This Spring Boot application has been
created for learning","name":"User Registration System
Application","version":"1.0.0"}}
```

Figure 7-9. *Customized health endpoint*

The /health endpoint gives health information that is collected from all the beans that implement a HealthIndicator interface and is configured in your application context. Since some of the information is sensitive in nature, you can configure endpoints.health.sensitive=false to expose other information such as the disk space and data source, as shown in Figure 7-10.

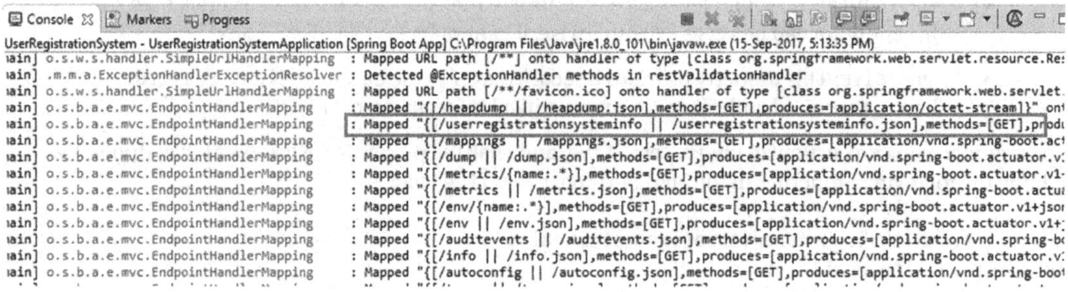

Figure 7-10. *Customized /info endpoint*

Similarly, you can customize the data shown by the /info endpoint by adding the following properties in the application.properties file:

```
info.app.name=User Registration System Application
info.app.description=This Spring Boot application has been created for learning
info.app.version=1.0.0
```

The following output will appear in the browser, as shown in Figure 7-9.

```
{
    "app":
    {
    "description":"This Spring Boot application has been created for learning",
    "name":"User Registration System Application",
    "version":"1.0.0"
    }
}
```

Custom Health Indicator

You can also define your own custom health indicator by implementing the HealthIndicator interface and overriding the unimplemented method. This custom health indicator collects any type of custom health data specific to the application and provides it to the /health endpoint. Listing 7-2 shows the CustomHealthIndicator class that implements the HealthIndicator interface.

Listing 7-2. CustomHealthIndicator Class

```
import org.springframework.boot.actuate.health.Health;
import org.springframework.boot.actuate.health.HealthIndicator;
import org.springframework.stereotype.Component;
```

```java
@Component
public class CustomHealthIndicator implements HealthIndicator {

        @Override
        public Health health() {
                int errorCode = check();
                if (errorCode == 0) {
                        return Health
                                .up()
                                .withDetail("Status", "UP")
                                .withDetail("Error Code", errorCode)
                                .withDetail("Description",
                                        "Your Custom Health indicator point is UP")
                                .build();
                }
                return Health.up().build();
        }

        public int check() {
                return 0;
        }
}
```

The following output will appear in the browser, as shown in Figure 7-11.

```json
{
        "status":"UP",
        "custom":{
                "status":"UP",
                "Status":"UP",
                "Error Code":0,
                "Description":"Your Custom Health indicator point is UP"
                },
        "diskSpace":{
                "status":"UP",
                "total":142753132544,
                "free":97823797248,
                "threshold":10485760
                },
        "db":{
                "status":"UP",
                "database":"H2",
                "hello":1
        }
}
```

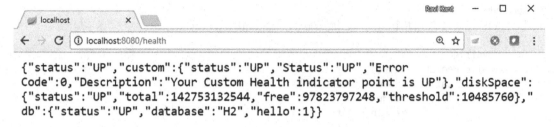

{"status":"UP","custom":{"status":"UP","Status":"UP","Error
Code":0,"Description":"Your Custom Health indicator point is UP"},"diskSpace":
{"status":"UP","total":142753132544,"free":97823797248,"threshold":10485760},"
db":{"status":"UP","database":"H2","hello":1}}

Figure 7-11. /health endpoint

Defining New Endpoints

Even though Spring Boot Actuator provides endpoints, you can define a new endpoint other than the existing Actuator endpoints. Let's create a new endpoint by creating the MyCustomEndpoint class and implementing the Endpoint<List<String>> interface, as shown in Listing 7-3.

Listing 7-3. MyCustomEndpoint Class

```
import java.util.ArrayList;
import java.util.List;

import org.springframework.boot.actuate.endpoint.Endpoint;
import org.springframework.stereotype.Component;

@Component
public class MyCustomEndpoint implements Endpoint<List<String>> {

        @Override
        public String getId() {
                return "myCustomEndpoint";
        }

        @Override
        public List<String> invoke() {
                List<String> customMessages = new ArrayList<String>();
                customMessages.add("This is custom message 1");
                customMessages.add("This is custom message 2");
                return customMessages;
        }

        @Override
        public boolean isEnabled() {
                return true;
        }

        @Override
        public boolean isSensitive() {
                return true;
        }

}
```

Let's run the Spring Boot application. The console log will contain the /myCustomEndpoint endpoint, as shown in Figure 7-12.

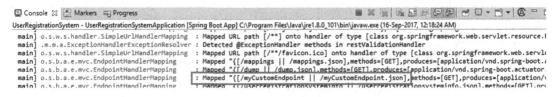

Figure 7-12. *New endpoints in the console*

You can access this new endpoint using its id value at /myCustomEndpoint. The output will display in the browser, as shown in Figure 7-13.

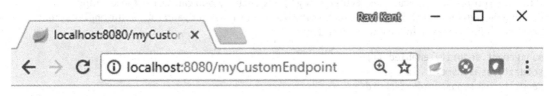

Figure 7-13. */myCustomEndpoint endpoint*

Management Over HTTP

In this section, you will manage the Actuator endpoint over HTTP.

Customizing the Server Port

You can customize the server port to expose the Actuator endpoint over a nonstandard port for security purposes. You can use the management.port property to configure this.

You can also change the address using the management.address property to restrict where the endpoint can be accessed from over the network.

Let's change the following properties in the application.properties file:

```
management.port=8081
management.address=127.0.0.1
```

When you restart the Spring Boot application and access the /health endpoint using the customized address and port number, the output will return, as shown in Figure 7-14.

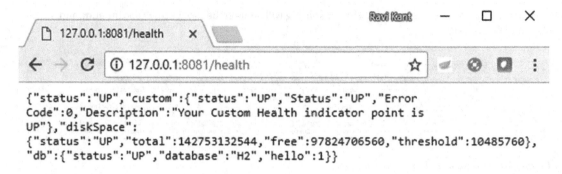

```
{"status":"UP","custom":{"status":"UP","Status":"UP","Error
Code":0,"Description":"Your Custom Health indicator point is
UP"},"diskSpace":
{"status":"UP","total":142753132544,"free":97824706560,"threshold":10485760},
"db":{"status":"UP","database":"H2","hello":1}}
```

Figure 7-14. *Customized port number and address*

Accessing a Sensitive Endpoint

When the Spring Boot application is secured using Spring Security, you can secure these endpoints by defining the default security properties, such as the username, password, and role, in the application. properties file, as shown in the following code:

```
management.security.enabled=true
security.user.name=admin
security.user.password=password
security.user.role=ADMIN
```

When you try to access the secured endpoint such as /info, which is sensitive by default, a pop-up will prompt for the credentials, as shown in Figure 7-15.

Figure 7-15. *Accessing a secured endpoint*

Summary

In this chapter, you learned about Spring Boot Actuator and how to enable Actuator by adding the dependency in the Maven pom.xml file. Then you saw a few Actuator endpoints. Later, you customized these existing Spring Boot Actuator endpoints and defined new endpoints. Finally, you customized the server port.

■ ■ ■

Tools for Accessing REST APIs

When you have to work in an agile development environment, you need to be able to quickly test your API. In this appendix, you will learn about open source REST API testing.

GUI testing for REST API services is slow and a poor choice for developers who want to get quick results about their code from the latest build. API testing is considered a better choice for developers because it tends to be faster and is more reliable than GUI testing.

API Testing

Application programming interface (API) testing involves bypassing the user interaction using a GUI/web page and communicating directly to the services within an application by making API calls.

API testing lets developers test "headless" technologies such as RESTful web services. In headless testing, the GUI (or head) is bypassed; requests are sent directly to an application's services, and the services receive responses to validate the results.

API Testing Tools

You will need to find a tool to do REST APIs testing. There are a number of API testing tools available on the Internet; for example, Selenium is a browser-based testing tool. In this book, you will be using Postman.

Let's explore the Postman API testing tools.

Postman

Postman is a REST client that started off as a Chrome browser plug-in for making HTTP requests. Postman can be used to make HTTP requests to REST services and get responses from the server.

You can download Postman from the Chrome web store using the link `https://chrome.google.com/webstore/detail/postman/fhbjgbiflinjbdggehcddcbncdddomop`, as shown in Figure A-1.

© Ravi Kant Soni 2017
R. K. Soni, *Full Stack AngularJS for Java Developers*, https://doi.org/10.1007/978-1-4842-3198-2

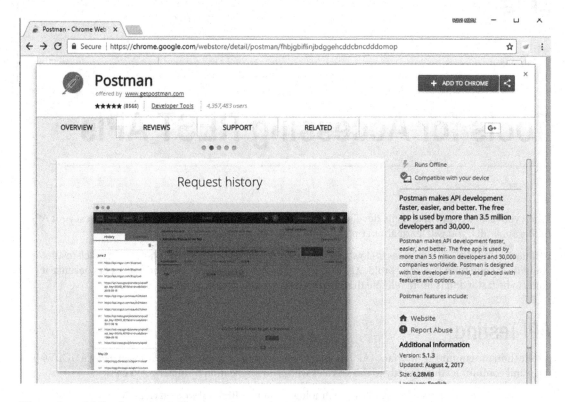

Figure A-1.   Adding Postman to Chrome

Clicking the Add To Chrome button will result in a pop-up, as shown in Figure A-2.

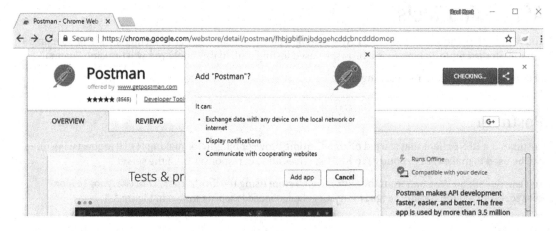

Figure A-2.   Pop-up to add Postman app

Clicking "Add app" will download a .crx file. Once this download is successful, Postman will be added to the Chrome app list. Visit chrome://apps/ in a Chrome browser to see the list of apps available in Chrome.

Now you can launch the app by clicking the Launch App button, as shown in Figure A-3.

Figure A-3. *Launching an app*

Once you launch the app, you will get a new window showing the Postman tool, as shown in Figure A-4.

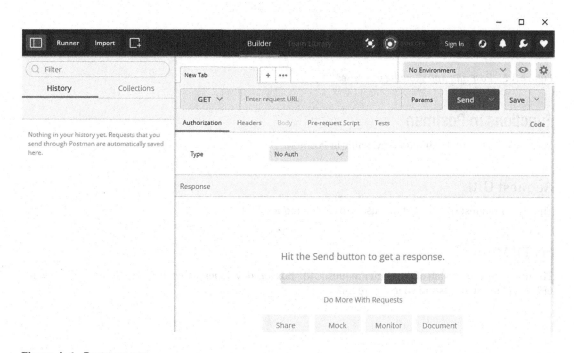

Figure A-4. *Postman app*

Postman lets developers compose HTTP requests from the user interface and send those requests to the server. Developers can view the responses, as shown in Figure A-5.

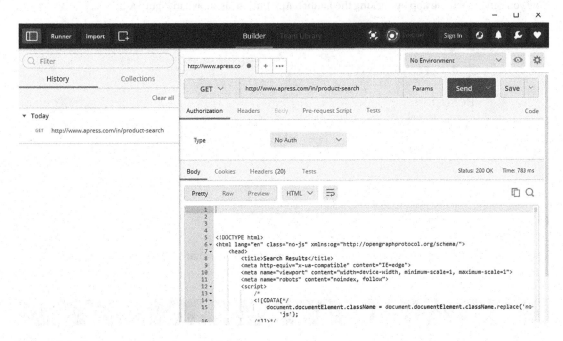

Figure A-5. *Postman app showing responses*

Functions in Postman

Let's look at a few of the functions available in Postman.

Request URL

The "Enter request URL" box allows users to enter a request URL.

HTTP Method

The drop-down to the left of the "Enter request URL" box lets developers select their HTTP method, such as GET, POST, and so on, as shown in Figure A-6.

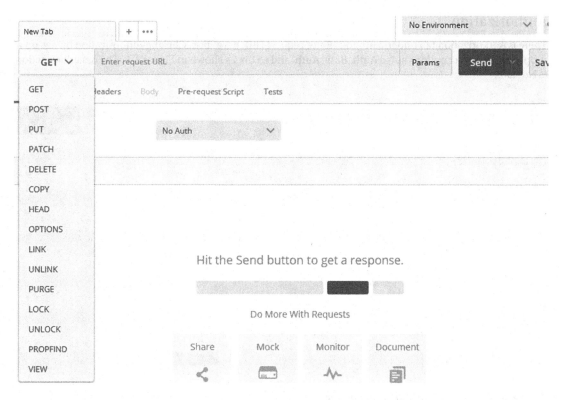

Figure A-6. *HTTP methods*

Parameters

The Params button is to the right of the "Enter request URL" box. This lets users set the param's key and value, which will be passed along with the request URL that calls an API, as shown in Figure A-7.

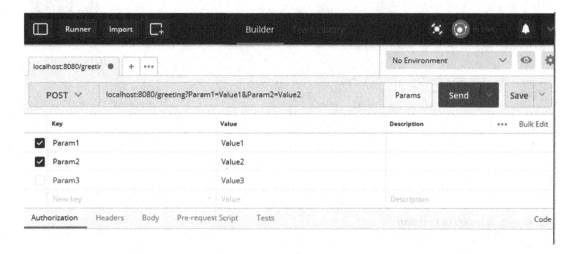

Figure A-7. *Parameters in Postman*

Authorization

There is Authorization tab underneath the "Enter request URL here" box. Clicking Authorization brings up a drop-down to select options as No Auth, Basic Auth, and so on, as shown in Figure A-8. The default selection is No Auth.

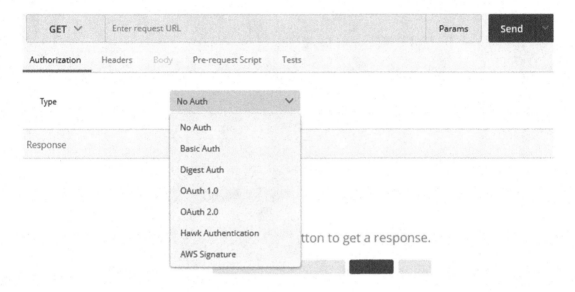

Figure A-8. *Authorization options in Postman*

Headers

Clicking Headers allows the user to enter header information, as shown in Figure A-9.

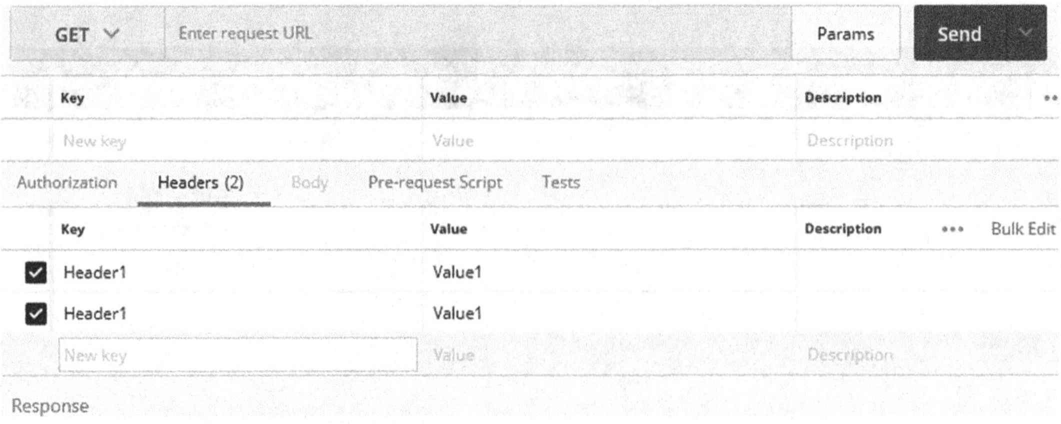

Figure A-9. *Headers in Postman*

Body

The Body tab is available only for these HTTP methods: Post, Put, Patch, Delete, Link, Unlink, Lock, and Propfind. For other HTTP methods, it will be disabled. Clicking Body will bring up four options: form-data, x-www-form-urlencoded, raw, and binary.

- *Form-data*: Selecting this will reveal a row with a Key drop-down menu.

- *X-www-form-urlencoded*: Selecting this will reveal a row below with Key and Value fields.

- *Raw*: Selecting this will reveal a drop-down menu and a text box with numbered rows, as shown in Figure A-10. The drop-down menu has the following options: Text, Text (text/plain), JSON (application/json), Javascript (application/javascript), XML (application/xml), XML (text/xml), and HTML (text/html).

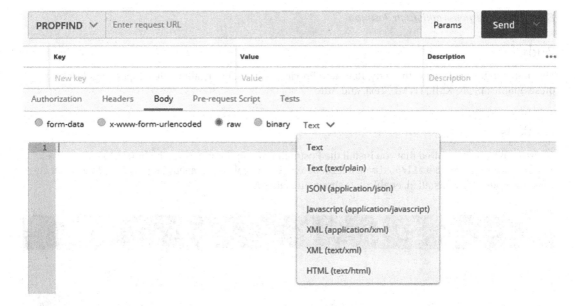

Figure A-10. *Body options in Postman*

Send

Use the blue Send button to send the HTTP request.

Response Message

After clicking the Send button, you'll receive a response message from requested APIs. The response message can include tabs called Body, Cookies, Headers, and Tests, as shown in Figure A-11.

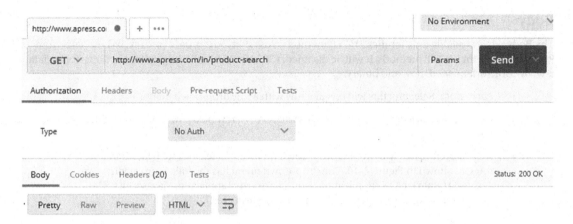

Figure A-11. *Response options in Postman*

Body

The body can be displayed with Pretty, Raw, and Preview options. Pretty allows developers to select from these options: JSON, XML, HTML, Text, and Auto.

Cookies

To use cookies, it is required that you install the Postman Interceptor app using the link `https://chrome.google.com/webstore/detail/postmaninterceptor/aicmkgpgakddgnaphhhpliifpcfhicfo?hl=en`. Once the Interceptor app is installed, enable it as shown in Figure A-12.

Figure A-12. *Enabling Interceptor for cookies*

Headers

This will display the headers received in the row format.

Tests

This is available for paid customers.

Other Features

The History section of Postman, on the left of the window, records all the requests you've made, as shown in Figure A-13. History saves the HTTP requests and allows them to be reopened.

Figure A-13. *History in Postman*

Index

Get the eBook for only $5!

Why limit yourself?

With most of our titles available in both PDF and ePUB format, you can access your content wherever and however you wish—on your PC, phone, tablet, or reader.

Since you've purchased this print book, we are happy to offer you the eBook for just $5.

To learn more, go to http://www.apress.com/companion or contact support@apress.com.

Apress®

Printed in the United States
By Bookmasters